2.75

ADVANCED
TENNIS

About the author

Chet Murphy, former tennis coach at the Univesity of California, is now co-ordinator of tennis instruction at the Berkeley campus. A former nationally ranked player, Murphy was runner-up for the NCAA singles and doubles tennis titles. He has coached collegiate tennis for twenty-four years in Chicago, Detroit, Minnesota, and California. During his ten years at the University of California, he coached five All-American players, and his teams were regularly among the strongest in the country, finishing third twice and fifth twice in NCAA play.

A long-time tennis professional at the Broadmoor Hotel in Colorado Springs, he is also a national organizer and conductor of frequent tennis workshops and clinics for players and teachers. He is a former president of the NCAA Tennis Coaches Association and former chairman of the AAHPER-USLTA Joint Committee for School Tennis Development.

In 1972, Murphy and his brother Bill, of the University of Arizona, received the USLTA's Educational Service Award in recognition of their work in clinics and workshops and for their committee positions and publications. Murphy is coauthor of *Tennis for Beginners* and *Tennis Handbook* (Ronald Press publications) and of *Tennis for the Player, Teacher, and Coach* (W. B. Saunders Co.).

ADVANCED TENNIS

Physical Education Activities Series

Chet Murphy
University of California
Berkeley

Second Edition

Wm C Brown Company Publishers
Dubuque, Iowa

Consulting Editor

Aileene Lockhart
Texas Woman's University

Evaluation Materials Editor

Jane A. Mott
Smith College

Copyright © 1970, 1976, by Wm. C. Brown Company Publishers

Library of Congress Catalog Card Number: 75-23608

ISBN 0—697—07070—0

Printed in the United States of America

Contents

Preface

As your interest in tennis grows and as you see more good players in action, you will become aware that several different methods are used to produce the various strokes. Perhaps you have already noticed different backswings, stances, finishes and even different grips. Perhaps you are already wondering about this, realizing that many good players play differently from the way you were originally taught. Do not let this disturb you. No two players play exactly alike, and yet many, many players play properly and efficiently. "But how can this be so?" you may ask. "What is correct? What is best?"

There is more than one correct way to play. There are several variations in the backswing and the finish, for example, that permit an efficient hit. The differences you have noticed in these and in other parts of the swing may all be proper and permissible, provided they fall within a certain range of correctness. Any method that permits the hitter to hit the ball efficiently must be considered correct and within the range of acceptable form. If, for example, a player whose style you admire holds the racket differently than you do, it may not mean your grip is bad and should be changed. If your grip lets you place your wrist and racket in the right position, and if it lets you use your arm, hips, and shoulders as they must be used to produce an efficient hit, then your grip is a good one, and you should continue to use it.

Quite possibly, too, the total pattern of your stroke may be just as proper and efficient as that of some better players you see, even though it differs from theirs. If you followed instructions carefully in your elementary classes, it is quite likely that you have a firm foundation on which to build. This is why you are reading this book; you are ready to move ahead. You are ready for more instruction and more practice so you can add refinements to your basic form. This book offers that instruction. Here you will be introduced to the more advanced techniques and tactics that will enable you to play at a notch higher on the ladder of tennis development than you now do.

You will not be expected to break down your present stroke patterns and to build new ones. Instead, you will be encouraged to build on what you already have by incorporating into your patterns certain points of form that are considered to be common fundamentals—things that most good players do. These fundamentals are essential for effective play at higher levels. The earlier you start working on them, the earlier you will be able to compete with players who now seem far beyond you in ability.

Self-evaluation questions are disturbed throughout this book. You should attempt to answer these and pose other suitable questions to yourself. This is the way to learn. Keep a check on your progress.

Although this book is addressed primarily to students who are enrolled in intermediate and advanced classes, the information is clearly appropriate for and useful to anyone who aspires to become an above-average tennis player.

Let's move ahead, now, to a discussion of refined and sophisticated stroke techniques, and to a consideration of effective tactics and strategy at intermediate and advanced levels.

The forehand ground stroke

1

Your elementary tennis instruction probably began with work on the forehand drive. Your first swings were made from that side, and you soon learned to start the rally (to make the feeder shot) with that stroke. That grip and swing probably seemed more natural to you than the backhand. Consequently, you may have favored the forehand in practice and play, and as a result you probably soon considered it to be your best stroke.

This is the proper beginning. You must have a good forehand, but to win consistently, even if only in middle-class play, you must be able to do more than simply rally with your forehand. You must be able to *control the rally*. You must be able to create an opening, to attack when an opening develops, and you must be able to use the forehand to defend. This ability comes only after you learn to make minor adjustments, variations, and refinements in the basic form you have already developed. The instructions offered here permit and encourage variations—they can be called permissible differences— that enable you to acquire the smoothness and fluency necessary to develop an all-purpose forehand. The directions are for right-handed players; left-handed players should reverse them.

GRIPPING THE RACKET

The Eastern Grip

When you were learning to play, you were probably told to shake hands with the racket to place your hand in the Eastern grip. Later instruction was probably more specific. The fleshy part of your hand at the base of the first and second fingers became a reference point, and you were told to place it against the large back plane of the handle.

Now, however, you don't need to feel restricted to this precise placement of your hand. Slight variations and adjustments are permissible, and you should experiment to see if any work better for you. If you feel more comfortable with your hand placed slightly toward either the top or bottom of the back plane, use that grip. You may also adjust your racket to make the back plane slant across your hand from the base of your forefinger to the heel of your palm, or you may hold the racket more in your fingers than in your palm. All of these variations are within the range of correctness, and all allow an efficient swing. Try them out to see which gives you a grip that feels firm and enables you to sense the position of your racket. When you find one that feels right, use it.

The Continental Grip

If you had a permissive teacher or if you are a self-taught player, you may now be using the Continental grip, in which the hand is placed more toward the top of the handle. This grip has the advantage of not requiring a change when hitting alternately at forehands and backhands and is therefore useful in net play where there isn't always time to change. It presents some problems, however, when used on ground strokes.

Because the plane of the palm is far out of line with the plane of the hitting face of the racket, it may be difficult for you to sense the slant of the hitting face as it makes contact with the ball. As a result, you may not have good up-and-down control of your shots. Secondly, the Continental grip requires a strong hand and forearm to prevent excessive wrist action in the swing. Wrist action adds speed to a shot, but it usually prevents a player from developing consistent left-to-right control. Therefore, if you have trouble controlling your shots, you should consider changing to the Eastern grip.

The Western Grip

Most self-taught players who started playing when they were young children seem to have adopted the Western grip naturally. For this grip the palm is placed under the handle rather than behind it or on top of it. With the hand supporting the racket from beneath, less strength is required to control the racket than in either of the other grips, and for many learners this is the overriding consideration. The Western grip is not common now in top-level play, however, because it requires a marked change from forehand to backhand, and in fast play there is not always time to make such a change.

However this grip has one excellent feature. It often enables a player to develop a fast, accurate top-spin drive—the type of drive that a player can rely on as a primary weapon. If your game is built around such a strong stroke, you should continue to use this grip, provided you can make the quick adjustment in grips necessary to hit backhands. If, on the other hand, your Western forehand is unsteady and inaccurate, you should practice changing your grip and stroke patterns to make them more closely approximate a true Eastern.

ADJUSTING THE WRIST POSITION

Whichever grip you choose, you must hold your racket firmly, especially at the moment of impact. You need a firm grip to move your racket quickly, to place it on the ball properly, and to resist the force of the oncoming ball.

You may avoid some problems that often develop at impact if you understand two points about the anatomical relationship between your grip and wrist.

1. When anything is gripped tightly in the hand, the movements of the wrist are restricted.
2. The greatest amount of grip strength can be attained when the wrist is in the middle position, in line with the forearm, rather than either cocked (so that the thumb points upward) or extended (so that the fingers point downward). (See fig. 1.1.)

Fig. 1.1.   With an Eastern forehand grip and the wrist in the middle position, as shown in the first frame, the racket handle is parallel to the ground. This is the ideal position for balls at waist height, but it is not always practical for lower balls. In the second frame the wrist is cocked in the manner typical of players who use the Continental grip. The rounded wrist position shown in the third frame does not provide as much racket control as either of the other positions.

When swinging at a high ball, therefore, do not cock your wrist beyond the middle position to raise your racket. Instead, raise your arm at the shoulder so that you can maintain the middle wrist position while raising your racket to the height of the ball.

When swinging at a low ball, do not extend your wrist to lower your racket. Instead, bend your knees and lower your arm at the shoulder so that you can maintain the efficient middle position of the wrist. On very low balls your racket face may be lower than your hand, but this is not important. The position of your wrist should be your main concern. Do not cock it or extend it; maintain a middle wrist position for firmness and control.

ADJUSTING YOUR HITTING STANCE

The ideal hitting stance is sideways, just as it is in baseball and golf. A line drawn from the rear foot to the front foot should run parallel to the intended line of flight of the ball. In such a stance, called a square stance, you are able

Of the three forehand grips, the Eastern is the most popular. Can you think of several reasons why fewer players choose to use the Continental or the Western grip?

to step in the general direction of the net as you swing. The step and transfer of weight is one of the main sources of power, and you should use it whenever necessary. Step with the left foot.

Unlike batters and golfers, however, in fast play you will not always have time to set yourself nicely into a sideways stance. You will have to stretch to the side for some balls and step away from others. This means that you will have to adjust your left-foot step, varying its direction to reach wide balls and to gain swinging room on close balls and still move your weight into the shot.

The most frequent need for such adjustments occurs when you are returning the serve. On a fast serve, you often will have time to make only one step, a crossover with the left foot, to reach wide balls. You will have to step sideways with your left foot rather than toward the net. When you swing from this position, your stance is called *closed.*

On fast serves hit directly at you, you will not always have time to move away from the ball and turn into the sideways stance. Instead, you may have time only to lean to your left and step away from the ball with your left foot as you swing. When you hit with your body facing the net this way, you are hitting from an *open* stance.

If a ball is hit close to you during a rally, you must move away to hit it. First, move your right foot back and slightly to your left. Then step with your left foot, adjusting the direction of your step to enable you to swing comfortably. You may have to hit from an open stance, but you still should transfer your weight to your left foot as you swing.

When you have to move to reach a wide ball during a rally, time your steps and adjust their number and size so you can set your left foot down just as you start your forward swing. Do not hit the ball while your left foot is in the air and you are in the middle of a step. Try, however, to get set near enough to the ball to enable you to step toward the net as you swing, even if your stance will be markedly open. In this situation and in others in which you do not need maximum speed and accuracy, the open stance may be more convenient, more comfortable, and more suitable than either of the other stances.

If you do have to make a big step toward the sideline with your left foot to reach the ball, try to turn your foot toward the net a bit as you place it. This move at least will allow you some body action as you swing; you will not block your hips out of the shot completely.

MAKING THE BACKSWING

Although you were taught to take your racket straight back and to pause before starting your forward swing, you should now learn to swing with continuous motion. In fast play you often will not have time to pause, and if you attempt to do so, you will develop a wristy shot. Even if you can avoid that, you will tighten up and as a result develop a stiff, rigid swing. Neither is desirable, and you should change your swing to avoid these faults.

You can have continuous motion with either a straight backswing or a circular one. If your swing is straight back, straighten your elbow a bit and make a slight downward, circular motion with your forearm as your racket begins to point toward the rear fence. This will be the start of a loop that will enable you to change from a backswing to a forward swing without stopping. The loop also permits you to adjust the racket to the height of the ball before you begin the forward swing.

Fig. 1.2. The forehand drive, showing the loop backswing, the step toward the net, the bent knees, the body rotation, the laid-back wrist, and the swing along the line toward the target.

Can you account in terms of mechanical principles for the relative advantages and disadvantages of the circular and the flat backswings? Should you adjust the speed of your backswing or the time at which you start the backswing in executing the forehand drive?

You may be more comfortable if you swing the racket back in a circular pattern. As you turn sideways from the ready position, release your left hand from the racket's throat and carry the racket upward and backward until it points toward the rear fence. Then straighten your elbow and continue with the loop action described previously. Trace an egg-shaped pattern with your racket, moving up and back, down and around, then forward into the ball.

As you make your backswing, you may keep your elbow down or you may raise it. Either method works, and both are used by ranking players. By keeping your elbow down, you can simplify your swing. This may be reason enough for keeping your elbow in this position; it will enable you to keep the racket face in the proper position at contact—flat, vertical, standing on edge. If you raise your elbow, the hitting surface of your racket will slant downward, and you will have to make adjustments in your elbow and wrist positions to bring the face into the ball properly. This is not the easiest and most efficient way to hit, but it will enable you to generate a great deal of racket speed. If you can manage to control this kind of swing, it may be the best kind for you.

Whichever method you use, start your backswing as soon as you determine the direction of the ball as it comes off your opponent's racket. If you merely have to turn to reach the ball, make the backswing as you turn. If you have to run to reach a wide ball, make the backswing while you are running. In either case, adjust the speed of your backswing to keep your motion continuous; swing quickly for a fast ball and slowly for a slow ball.

MAKING THE FORWARD SWING

Whenever possible, step toward the net with your left foot just before your racket reaches the lowest part of the loop in your backswing. Finish the loop as you step, and turn your hips and shoulders counterclockwise to start your forward swing. Swing your arm at the shoulder to guide the racket into the ball. If you intend to hit a flat shot, swing the racket in a fairly flat plane. For a top-spin shot, swing in an upward plane.

In intermediate and advanced play, you often will need top spin on your ground strokes. Top spin permits you to hit the ball hard and still keep it in the court. It also enables you to keep the ball low, near your opponent's feet. You can attack with it, pass with it, and play defensively with it. Learn to use it for all of these purposes.

There are three ways to put top spin on the ball. The easiest to learn, and the most efficient and reliable way, is to hit up on the ball with a vertical racket face, brushing the back side of the ball in an upward motion. As you lower your racket during your loop, straighten your arm as much as is necessary to place the racket below the intended height of contact. Then swing

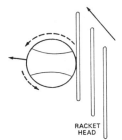

Fig. 1.3 Sketch shows what happens at contact—from the hitter's viewpoint—on a forehand top-spin drive. The upward-moving racket hits the ball a glancing blow, and as a result, the ball has top spin.

RACKET HEAD

forward and upward into the ball. You may accentuate the upward swing by straightening your knees during the forward swing and increase the racket speed by whipping the racket face upward with a flexible wrist.

A second way is to lift and bend your elbow slightly as your racket comes into contact with the ball. As your elbow comes up, it will cause the hitting face of your racket to close* a little and to turn the ball over. This motion requires precise timing, but it is an efficient way to apply top spin to a high, bouncing ball. On low balls, however, the closed racket face almost always causes an error in the net.

A third way to apply top spin is to rotate your wrist and forearm at contact to roll your racket face over the ball. This is an easy way to spin the ball, but it is not easy to control because of the precise timing required as the racket changes positions.

THE POINT OF CONTACT

The point of contact on any particular shot is determined by the kind of grip you use and by the direction toward which you intend to hit. If your grip is a true Eastern, your point of contact to hit straight ahead will be approximately opposite your left hip. If your grip is closer to a Western, meet the ball sooner (closer to the net). If your grip is closer to a Continental, meet the ball later (farther from the net). If you intend to hit crosscourt to your left, meet the ball sooner than you would for a straight-ahead shot. If you intend to hit to your right meet the ball a bit later.

By adjusting your timing this way, you can place your racket either directly on the back side of the ball (the side farthest from the net) or slightly toward either the far or near side of it. In advanced play, however, it often will be advantageous or necessary to make quick wrist adjustments rather than to rely on precise timing to place your racket on the ball properly. You will then often be able to disguise the direction of your shot and even make defensive shots on balls that are difficult to position or time accurately. However you do it—whether by swinging sooner or later, or by making wrist adjustments—it may help if you think of making your racket's hitting surface face your target at impact.

*When the hitting face of the racket is slanted toward the ground, it is described as "closed"; when the hitting face slants toward the sky, it is described as "open."

Fig. 1.4 By adjusting the timing of the swing to meet the ball sooner or later, the player hits the ball to his left, straight ahead, and to his right. In fast play, however, split-second wrist adjustments are often necessary for control of direction.

LAYING THE WRIST BACK

Although as a beginner you were told to restrict wrist action in your swing, you should now begin to use it for placement and speed. This is not to say that your wrist should be loose and floppy. You should strive for a kind of controlled hand action that is a compromise between looseness and stiffness at the wrist.

As you start your backswing, lay your wrist back slightly to make an angle between your hand and forearm. Then, as you make your forward swing, reverse your wrist slightly to bring your hand more into line with your forearm. At impact you will want your racket face facing your target, so you must time this wrist action carefully. Firm up your wrist as your racket passes through the hitting area, and keep it that way through most of your follow-through.

SWINGING ALONG THE LINE

Because the ball compresses and the racket strings "give" a little at contact, the ball and strings stay in contact with each other longer than they would if they were solid objects. It is possible to use this "cushioning" effect to get maximum control of your ground strokes. To do this, your racket must be facing your target at impact, and it must be moving toward the target as it passes through the hitting area. Swing your racket along the intended line of flight of the ball.

The swing along the line is easy to learn. As your racket moves into the ball, move your elbow past your right hip and away from your body in the

What two adjustments are recommended for control of direction on the fore-hand? What kind of swing plane for top spin?

direction of your shot. In this way you will be able to straighten the path of the racket as it moves through the contact area. This is preferable to making a circular swing around your body, because the circular path permits only an instant hit. The straight path, on the other hand, lets you maintain contact for a fraction of a second longer. As you meet the ball, try to prolong contact— think of hitting the ball for a long time. At contact, guide your racket along the intended line of flight of the ball.

SWINGING FOR POWER

To hit accurately, you must tailor your swing to each particular situation. One of the variables you must consider is the amount of force to apply in your swing. Reviewing the sources of force and considering how they may be used may help you decide how much force is necessary.

On the forehand you can generate racket speed by (1) swinging your arm at the shoulder, (2) transferring your body weight from the right foot to the left foot, (3) turning your upper body clockwise during the backswing and counterclockwise during the forward swing, and (4) using some wrist action, or more properly, controlled hand action.

The degree to which you use these sources of force should be determined by the purpose of your shot. When you intend to drive a shot the full length of the court and at good speed, try to use all of the sources available. When you intend to return a fast serve to the feet of a net-rushing server, however, you may not need all of them; perhaps body rotation or the weight shift could be eliminated. With arm and elbow action alone, you may be able to supply enough force to fulfill your intention.

THE FINISH POSITION

Most of your drive swings will be made in an upward plane; your racket will be moving upward and forward as it comes into the ball. At the finish of your stroke, therefore, your racket will be high, sometimes face high or even higher.

The precise finish point will be determined by your intention to hit a high or low shot, a top-spin shot or a flat one. When you swing markedly upward to apply a great deal of top spin, you may be looking under your arm at the finish of your swing. When you hit flat or with only a little top spin, you may be looking over your arm at the finish (see fig. 1.2).

The length of your swing will be determined by the amount of force you apply to it. If you intend to hit softly, you should swing easily, and you may stop your racket when it is pointing straight ahead. When you apply a great deal of force to hit hard, however, you may not be able to stop your racket until it has moved off to your left. In either case, let your finish be a natural outcome of your swing. Use it as a checkpoint, a reference, to see if you swung in the proper plane, with the proper amount of force, and with your racket set properly for the height, speed, and direction you wanted.

ADJUSTING THE VARIABLES

In elementary tennis you practiced to "groove" you stroke, to produce the same pattern time after time. In advanced play, however, you must adjust your stroke to various conditions of play. On one particular shot, for example, you may be farther from the net, or the ball may bounce higher than on the preceding one. You may be aiming at your opponent's service line on one shot and closer to his baseline on another. Your strokes must differ on all of these shots. To drive a high-bouncing ball sharply downward, your racket face must be closed slightly, and your racket must be swung in a downward plane. To drive a low ball upward, your swing must be in an upward plane and/or your racket face must be open to provide enough lift for the ball to clear the net. Setting these variables accurately (the slant and angle of the racket face and the plane and force of the swing) is more important than producing a classic swing pattern time after time.

One good way to practice adjusting the variables is to aim at a fixed target (the cans in which balls are sold serve well for this purpose) from various locations in your court. You'll soon learn that it takes a higher as well as a stronger shot to hit the target when stroking from behind the baseline than when stroking from close to the service line. Also, to hit higher or lower, you must adjust the slant of your racket and/or the plane of your swing.

By learning to anticipate the conditions under which you are going to have to hit the oncoming ball, you are more likely to set the variables properly for a particular shot. Among the cues to look for are the force of your opponent's swing, the sound of impact, and the trajectory of the oncoming ball. You can then learn to predict what amount of force and what kind of trajectory you will need to return his shot.

HITTING WITH BALANCE

Hitting with good balance is one of the keys to accuracy. It reduces sideways movement and thus eliminates one of the variables you would otherwise have to contend with during your swing.

The clue to good balance is stepping properly, that is, in the right direction, with the left foot. One way to learn to hit with balance is to pose for a count or two after each swing, before recovering to the waiting position. If you can't do so, it is probably because you stepped in the wrong direction and got caught either too close or too far away from the ball.

When running for a wide shot, try to get to the ball in time to set yourself in a balanced hitting stance. You are more likely to be able to do this if you hurry to the ball. Try to get there ahead of time so you can slow down or even before you swing. The rhythm of these moves should be fast-slow, not slow-fast.

If you do not have time to stop before hitting, at least try to place the left foot down before contacting the ball in order to reduce the amount of sideways movement. You may not be able to pose on balance after your hit, but at least you will have reduced sideways movement to a minimum.

In fast play when your opponent hits hard and deep, you will not always have time to set yourself into a good hitting stance. Instead, you will have to hit while moving away from the net. As the ball approaches, turn and skip sideways toward the rear fence. Time and adjust your moves so you can start your swing as you push off with the right foot on one of your skips. Make a vigorous body turn while your feet are off the ground. Since you can't use all the normal sources of power in your swing (you can't step in and you can't shift your weight), use more of whatever you can. In this case it's more force in your body turn. In a sense, you will be hitting off balance but in a controlled way. Though this is not ideal, this move makes the best of a bad situation.

Fig. 1.5 Hitting while moving away from the net. Not having time to set herself into a good hitting position, the player jumps backward as she swings and uses vigorous body rotation to generate force in her swing.

The backhand ground stroke

2

There is a strange paradox about the backhand: players of average ability feel that it is the more diffcult of the two ground strokes, yet most tournament players feel more comfortable and more natural on the backhand than on the forehand. During your elementary instruction you probably felt uneasy in your first tries at backhands, too. The naturalness that tournament players feel on the backhand was not always there either. It had to be learned. Now you are ready to resume the practice and training that will enable you to develop as much confidence and poise when hitting from the left side as from the right. The instructions offered here permit minor variations in style but require strict attention to basic patterns of form.

GRIPPING THE RACKET

The requirements for a good backhand grip are similar to those for the forehand. It should feel comfortable, it should be strong enough to permit you to move the racket quickly and to resist the force of the oncoming ball, and it should enable you to sense the position, the slant, of your racket face. Experiment wth your grip to find the placement of your hand that provides these features.

If you now use an Eastern or Western forehand grip, you should change it for backhands. Move your hand counterclockwise toward the top of the handle. If you use the Continental grip, you will not have to change it between forehands and backhands. This no-change feature is a big advantage in fast play, and, for that reason the Continental grip is used by most ranking players for net play. Many use it for ground strokes, too.

A reference point for discussing the backhand grip is the large knuckle at the base of your forefinger. Place it on the top plane of your handle or on the bevel to the right of it. Wrap your fingers around the handle and spread your first and second fingers slightly. You may either wrap your thumb around the handle or extend it along the back of it; both methods are correct. If you prefer the latter, adjust your hand so that the thumb and forefinger extend an equal distance along the handle so that an imaginary line through your large knuckles slants across the top of the handle. If your thumb extends along the handle alone (in which case your knuckles will be parallel to the handle), you will have a tendency to roll your wrist and forearm on low balls, and the result will be poor ball control.

The critical point about the backhand grip is the position of the wrist. If it is in front of the handle, you can only pull your racket toward the ball. If your hand is on top of the handle, or nearly so, you will have more of a feelng of pushing the racket. This will provide more strength and therefore more racket control, as well as more force in the swing. Adjust your grip so that your hand is placed near enough to the top of the handle to move your wrist away from the front of it.

Keep a firm grip throughout the entire stroke, and cock your wrist enough to avoid the weak, rounded-wrist position. For low balls, you will have to bend your knees to prevent the racket from dangling loosely. For high balls, cock your wrist to raise the racket as you raise your arm at the shoulder. When your hand is in the backhand palm-down position, you can hold the racket more firmly with a slightly cocked wrist than with a middle wrist position.

Fig. 2.1 For maximum racket control on the backhand, the wrist should be cocked slightly, as shown in the first frame. The weak, rounded-wrist position shown in the second frame usually results in poor racket control.

ADJUSTING THE HITTING STANCE

The most efficient hitting stance is sideways to the net. But here, as on the forehand, you will not always be able to set yourself into such a stance, and you should not attempt to do so in all situations. If you are returning a serve, for example, and your intention is to hit low to the feet of a server who is rushing the net, the open stance, with your body facing the net, may be adequate. You may not have time or the need to move your feet except to pivot on them so that you can rotate your body at least slightly as you swing.

Whenever possible, however, you should step into the shot with your right foot as you swing. Whether rallying or returning serves, make whatever adjustments are necessary as you step with that foot. Step toward the left sideline to reach a wide ball; step toward the right sideline or right net post to get away from a close one. When the ball is nicely alongside of you, step toward the net. In these three positions your stances can be described successively as *closed*, *open*, and *square*.

When you have to run to reach a ball, move with little steps so that your last step—the one just before contact—can be made with your right foot. Here again, your stance may be closed, open, or square, depending on how close you get to the ball.

In advanced play you often will have to hit while your weight is on your rear foot or even while you are moving or jumping sideways toward the rear fence. When you do, you will not be able to use all the normal sources of power in your swing. You must compensate then and use more of whatever sources are available. On the backhand you can use elbow action regardless of how you stand. In the difficult situations described here, you should straighten your arm vigorously at the elbow as if making a karate chop. Often, however, a defensive shot is even more suitable. It may be best to slice deep to an opponent playing the baseline or a short and low shot to the feet of an opponent playing close to the net. For these you would not have to step into the shot, transfer your weight, or use body rotation as you would when hitting from an ideal stance. You could simply use arm and elbow action.

MAKING THE BACKSWING

As on the forehand, your backswing may be straight or circular. The straight swing can be made faster, so you should use it when you have to swing quickly, for example, when you must return a fast serve.

On the loop, however, it is possible to make a smooth transition from the backswing to the forward swing that is more efficient mechanically; thus, you should use it whenever possible. To make the loop, raise your forearm (with the racket) and move it backward across your lower chest. As the racket begins to point toward the rear fence, lower your forearm and bring the racket handle in toward your left hip. With your hitting hand moving down and to the rear of your left hip, you have started your loop.

Generally, your loop should be shallow, but it must be adjusted and varied according to the height of the ball. On high balls, instead of circling down around the left hip, the hitting hand should be brought in close to the left elbow. For extremely high balls it may be closed to your shoulder. For low balls it must dip down below your left hip to enable you to swing upward into the ball. When your hand is close to either your hip, elbow, or shoulder, your arm is bent at the elbow. Straighten your arm during the forward swing to add elbow action to total arm action as a source of power.

Fig. 2.2   In the backhand ground stroke, the left hand pulls the racket face back from the ready position to facilitate changing grips. The backswing is a slight circular motion. The hitting arm, bent during the backswing, straightens at impact. The follow-through is forward, along the line of flight of the ball.

MAKING THE FORWARD SWING

Adjust the depth of your loop to enable you to start your forward swing below the height at which you intend to contact the ball. Close your right hand firmly on the handle and simply swing the racket out of your left hand.

Start the forward swing by stepping with the right foot and shifting your weight to it. Turn your hips and shoulders and swing your arm from the shoulder as you step. The elbow action described earlier should be part of your arm swing; for maximum power, straighten your arm vigorously as you swing.

Just as in the case of the forehand, the plane of the forward swing depends on the effect wanted at contact. For a top-spin shot, swing in an upward plane and meet the ball with either a vertical or slightly closed racket face. The more sharply upward you swing, the more top spin you will apply. You can accentuate the upward swing for a great deal of spin by straightening your knees as you hit. For a flat shot, swing in a level plane for high balls and in only a slightly upward plane for low balls. For a slice, move your racket in a downward plane as it passes through the hitting area. Your racket face may be flat to make contact with the back of the ball, or it may be opened slightly to place it a bit toward the bottom of the ball, depending on what kind of trajectory you want in your shot. For a lob, for example, you will need to slant your hitting surface markedly skyward to place it under the ball.

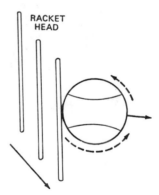

RACKET HEAD

Fig. 2.3 Sketch shows what happens at contact— from the hitter's point of view—on a backhand slice. The downward moving racket hits the ball a glancing blow, and as a result, the ball has backspin.

For very low balls, bend your knees as you start the forward swing so you can get the racket face down to the ball without changing your wrist angle. Keep your back straight and squat down to the ball just as if you were sitting down into a chair. Spread your legs, however, to maintain balance. The lower the ball, the more you will have to bend your knees, and the more you bend, the more you will have to spread. Keep a wide stance from which you can pivot and swing. A narrow stance prevents you from transferring your weight into the shot.

You will not be able to bend your knees and shift your weight properly if your rear heel remains on the ground. Life your heel and keep only the front part of your foot on the ground. This will encourage you to lean on your right foot as you swing, and soon you will develop a feeling of going to meet the ball, something all good strokers do.

THE POINT OF CONTACT

The point at which different players contact the ball varies as much as their grips do. It varies for a particular player, too, depending on the intended direction of his shot. If you want to hit straight ahead, you must place your racket squarely on the back side of the ball (the side farthest from the net). Experiment in practice to find the point opposite your body at which you can do this comfortably without making unusual or awkward adjustments with your wrist or elbow. Time your arm and elbow action so that your arm is straight at the point of contact. If you use wrist action (or more properly, controlled hand action that is the reverse of that used on the forehand), you must time it so that your racket face moves toward the target at impact.

To hit to your left, time your arm and elbow action so that you meet the ball a little later, while your arm is still slightly bent. This will enable you to place your racket slightly toward the near side of the ball while your racket moves toward your target.

To hit to your right, straighten your arm just before contact and meet the ball early enough to enable you to place your racket slightly toward the far side of the ball. Again, think of going to meet the ball and making your racket face move toward your target.

Hold your racket firmly, especially at impact. Cock your wrist a bit to create a slight angle between your racket handle and your forearm. You should keep this wrist position on all backhands, high or low, because it offers more strength and racket control than a straight wrist does. Equally important, it enables you to swing upward through the contact point to the finish.

During the backswing, this angled wrist position naturally turns the racket face slightly skyward. For this reason the backhand can be called an open-faced shot. As your racket comes into the ball, however, you should adjust your wrist to provide whatever slant of the racket face you want at contact. Even though you eventually may "groove" your stroke, you must contend with the slant of the racket at contact on every shot; it is part of feel and touch, two important requirements for controlled hitting.

THE FOLLOW-THROUGH

Control also comes from guiding your racket toward your target as it passes through the hitting area. To do this effectively, you must time and control your body rotation. Whenever possible, your upper body should be turning clockwise during your forward swing. When hitting from a closed or square stance, however, your shoulders should be turned sideways to the net until after you have hit the ball. Turning your body so that your chest faces the net before you hit may cause you to pull your racket across the line of flight

---

Use a square stance and a flat, straight-ahead backhand hit as a frame of reference. When would you open the racket face? When would you widen your stance? When would you delay your contact with the ball?

---

of the ball. Do not let the racket swing across the line until you are well into your follow-through. At contact, try to keep the racket on the ball for more than just a split second. Try to "stay with the ball" and guide it as it leaves your racket.

THE FINISH

On backhand drives your racket should finish high and slightly to your right. On chops and slices, in which the forward swing is in a downward rather than an upward plane, the finish is lower than the height of the ball at contact. Your hips and shoulders should have turned during the swing to change your upper body position from sideways at contact to facing the net at the finish.

Hold your finish position for one or two counts to check your balance. Balance is an aid to good hitting. It is related to footwork and timing and is seen best at the finish of your stroke. If your balance is "off," you should check your distance from the ball, your weight transfer, and your body position. You may discover that you stepped in the wrong direction just as you swung and either had to stretch to reach a wide ball or lean back from a close one. Either mistake can throw you off balance and break the pattern of your swing. Learn to pose on balance after your swing. You will not be able to pose in actual play, of course, because you will have to recover to the ready position, but in practice be a poser; hold a high firm finish.

WATCHING THE BALL

Since balance is related to stance and position, you must watch the ball carefully to judge it accurately in flight and on the bounce. Watch it leave your opponent's racket, look at it in flight, and watch it as you hit. You probably will not be able to see it on the strings of your racket because the action is too fast at that point, but you should be trying to do so. If the placement of your shots is off just slightly, it may be because you are neglecting to watch the ball as closely as you should. By correcting this, you may improve your judgment and timing.

THE TWO-HANDED BACKHAND

A review of the history of tennis shows that there have been two-handed hitters since the game was introduced in the United States in 1874. Until recently, however, the two-handed shot was considered unorthodox and was not usually taught by professional instructors. However, since several charismatic youngsters recently have been successful with two-handed backhands, the shot has become popular and acceptable with all except the most dogmatic teachers.

Fig. 2.4 Jim McManus, a world-class left-handed player, demonstrates his two-handed backhand. Note that the two-handed grip shortens his backswing and that he applies vigorous body rotation to attain force in his swing.

Most good two-handed hitters admit that they started that way because they could not control the racket adequately with one hand on their "weak" side. A few, however, simply found it more natural to swing that way because of previous two-handed hitting experiences in childhood games. If you are unhappy with your backhand and are progressing more slowly than on the forehand, experiment with a two-handed swing. If you find you have a reasonable amount of dexterity and sensitivity with your left hand, it may be wise to continue to use it to support your right hand (the reverse is true for left-handed players).

There are several different ways to hold the racket for a two-handed backhand. You may place your right hand toward the top of the handle in a typical Eastern or Continental backhand grip, or you may keep your hand in your usual Eastern forehand position. In the latter case, when you swing from your left side, your wrist will be in front of the handle (a weak position), but by supporting it with your left hand, you compensate for that weakness.

The position of the left hand also may vary. The usual procedure is to place it next to the right hand, closer to the strings, in either an Eastern, Continental, or Western position, depending on which gives more strength and control of the racket and more sensitivity to its position. All of these variations are used successfully by different two-handed hitters and may work for you.

Regardless of how you place your hands, your reach will be restricted somewhat if you try to keep both hands on the racket. Many wide balls will be unplayable unless you release your weaker hand and swing one-handed.

On a two-handed swing, you may use the normal sources of power—arm and elbow action, body rotation, and transfer of weight. But here you also may use a kind of double wrist action to help generate racket speed. You can also make your hands work against each other in a kind of "couple" arrangement.

As you swing, push against the handle with your right hand to momentarily fix it in place. At the same time, push against the handle with your left hand to cause the racket to swing in a circular path around your right hand. Such opposing forces applied at different points along the handle will increase the speed of the racket. You also may use the couple action to move your racket in a diagonal plane to force your racket upward quickly for the purpose of imparting top spin to the ball.

For maximum control, however, you should keep your left wrist in the typical laid-back position as if you were hitting a left-handed forehand. Use your left hand chiefly to support your right hand. Move your hands together toward the target area to move the racket along the intended line of flight of the ball. Then you will be able to prolong contact the way controlled hitters do.

The serve

3

In your first attempts at serving, you concentrated chiefly on getting the ball in play. Your objective was simply to avoid double faults. Now, however, you must do more with your serve than simply start a rally. You must be able to attack or at least play your opponent evenly on both your first and second balls.

At your present level of development, the most consistently effective serve is a spin serve—one with a combination of top spin and sidespin. Such a serve can be used as a first and second serve. You can learn to place the ball to your opponent's backhand with at least enough speed to prevent him from attacking on his return. Then later, as you gain control and confidence, you can change your wrist angle and racket path to hit your first ball more flatly. Even if you miss as many first serves as you make, you can follow with your reliable spin serve and still not be in trouble.

THE GRIP

The grip recommended for serving is the Continental, with the hand placed on the diagonal plane between the top and back planes of the handle. Almost all good servers use it or some slight variation of it because it permits wrist action and wrist adjustments at contact. Wrist action is necessary for power. Wrist adjustments are necessary for control, to permit you to vary the amount of spin on the ball, and to allow you to serve flat when you want to.

If you play with an Eastern or Western grip, the Continental may feel awkward and uncomfortable for serving. If so, try a slight variation of it. Adjust your forehand grip slightly to place the handle more in your fingers, with your palm almost completely off the racket. With that slight change, your grip will resemble the Continental and yet be more comfortable. In addition, you will have more freedom to use a quick finger action just before contact to get more racket speed and thus more spin and speed on the ball.

With either the Continental grip or the variation described above, you will have a natural tendency to put spin on the ball. You can feel this by placing your racket up at the contact point. It will feel almost as if you will hit the ball on the edge of the frame. Simply by turning your forearm to make your palm face the net, however, you can get the frame out of the way and place the strings on the ball.

An additional adjustment to consider is the long, butt-in-the-hand grip. Slide your hand down and almost off the end of the handle to place the butt in your palm. This, too, may permit you to generate more racket speed. If control rather than speed is your objective, however, you should hold your racket in the conventional manner, with the handle butt extending beyond your hand.

THE STANCE

The most efficient stance for serving is sideways to the net with your feet placed on an imaginary line pointing toward your target. Make whatever slight adjustments are needed, however, to make yourself comfortable. Find a stance that permits full body action so that you can shift your weight, bend and straighten your knees, and turn your hips and shoulders as you swing. To this end, you may place your rear foot to either the right or left of the reference line. Point your front foot toward the net post (not toward the sideline) to permit full body rotation as you swing.

Use your stance as a base from which to generate body rotation and upward body and arm action. You may find it helpful to slide your rear foot up to your front foot as you toss the ball; you will then be building a kind of two-footed platform from which to generate vigorous upward thrust as you swing. Bend your knees as the rear foot slides forward, and as you begin your upward swing, straighten them again for power.

THE TOSS

Toss the ball straight up in front of you so that you can meet it at a point slightly in front of your body. Tall players are able to meet the ball farther in front of themselves than shorter ones and still get a good angle down into the service court. Experiment to find your ideal point of contact. As a convenient guide for your toss, try to throw the ball so that if it fell to the ground, it would land in front of you on a line running from your feet toward your opponent.

If you are having toss problems in practice and play, it may help if you select one of the vertical fence posts behind your opponent and use it as a guide. As you toss, you should see the post in the periphery of your vision and guide your hand and the ball up the post.

You also may correct a faulty toss by watching yourself make the toss. Instead of looking up to where you intend to toss, as most good players do, or at a distant fence post, as recommended in the preceding paragraph, look at your tossing hand. See it go down and up, all the way up to face height before releasing the ball. You may find that this method gives you better control of your tossing arm; as a result, your tosses become more accurate.

Fig. 3.1   A good service swing showing the four check points: the racket moves past the knee, up toward the top of the rear fence, forward and behind the back, then up and into the ball. This server simply steps across the line, though either of the jump variations described in the text often provides more force in the swing (see Footwork When Serving, page 27).

THE SWING

Start your serve by standing sideways and holding the racket in front of you, pointing in the direction of the shot. Place the ball against the racket, either at the strings, the throat, or the handle. Sight through or above the racket, play the shot in your mind, and get a mental image of the ball going in as you want it to.

From the starting position, make your racket travel down past your right knee, up toward the top of the rear fence, in toward your back, and then up into the ball. Make your upward swing a natural throwing motion. Flip your wrist and fling the racket up toward the ball. Let your weight flow smoothly from back foot to front foot as you swing. Look at the ball, and time your swing to hit it when your arm is fully extended.

There are permissible variations in serving that you should experiment with. Although in a mechanical sense the racket path described here is most efficient, it may not be practical for you, particularly regarding the length of the backswing. You need not swing the racket back fully toward the rear fence before bringing it forward toward your back. Instead, you may bend your arm at various places in the arc of your backswing to move the racket toward the back-scratching position.

Fig. 3.2   Sketch shows permissible variations in the backswing when serving. The arm may be bent at various points along the arc (at 1, 2, 3, 4, or 5), though the long, full swing shown here is most efficient. Note that the palm is down until the racket begins to drop behind the hitter's back. This too is more efficient than a palm-up swing that causes the hitter to press his elbow against his side during the backswing.

A second adjustment that you can make during the backswing is in the position of your hitting hand and, with it, the elbow. You may raise your elbow and keep your hitting hand in the knuckles-up position in which you started your swing, or you may turn your hand clockwise to make the palm face skyward. The latter move will keep your elbow lower and closer to your side than the knuckles-up-swing.

The first method is the more common of the two because it usually results in better control. The wrist and forearm are not rotated or pronated during the backswing. Instead, they remain as they were in the starting position and as they will be at contact. As a result, the palm of the hitting hand faces skyward only when the player lowers the racket behind his back.

SPINNING THE BALL

The Basic Spin Serve

For an effective and consistent second serve, the ball must have overspin to make it curve downward as it clears the net. It is difficult to apply only overspin, however; spin serves are almost always a combination of overspin and sidespin.

An imaginary face on the ball provides reference points for the proper placement of the racket on the ball. For the basic spin serve, the racket should hit the face on the nose while moving toward the left eye. This can be done by curling the wrist just as your racket meets the ball (figure 3.3). The racket will then hook around the top right side of the ball and thus apply the appropriate spin.

Fig. 3.3   An imaginary face on the ball provides reference points for placing the racket properly on the ball when serving. For a spin serve, make contact on the nose while simultaneously curling the wrist (as shown by the arrow) to make the racket move toward the left eye.

The "American Twist" Serve

To apply a great deal of top spin and a moderate amount of sidespin, as in the "American twist" serve, you must toss the ball to your left and behind you, and you must bend backward in that direction to reach the ball. Reach back and around the ball to make contact on the right cheek of the imaginary face while your racket is moving up and across the line of flight from left to right. Straighten your back, arm, and wrist as the racket approaches the ball. Make contact with the ball before you reach the limit of your full upward extension. Whip the racket through the contact point, and carry the ball upward as you straighten your arm and wrist. Your racket should continue upward after contact. This may sound terribly complicated, but three cues may help simplify the process: (1) toss the ball to your left and behind you; (2) arch your back to reach the ball; and (3) hit up and across the ball.

When the spin is applied properly—making the ball spin on an imaginary diagonal axis—and the serve is aimed accurately, the ball will bounce fast and high to a receiver's backhand. The "American twist" serve is usually used for that purpose.

Fig. 3.4 The most reliable kind of spin for serving is a combination of top spin and sidespin that makes the ball rotate on an imaginary diagonal axis as shown.

THE FLAT SERVE

In addition to developing a reliable spin serve, you also should develop a hard, flat one. For such a serve, toss the ball straight up and high enough to hit when your arm and wrist are extended fully. Stretch upward and forward to get maximum reach at contact and to make the racket almost a direct extension of your arm.

Fig. 3.5 For a flat serve, the ball is tossed in front of the right shoulder, and there is only a slight angle between the racket handle and the forearm.

Fig. 3.6 For an "American twist" serve, the ball is tossed to the left and behind the server, causing him to bend backwards in that direction to reach it. The player hits up and across the ball, swinging from left to right.

During the upward swing, turn your wrist and forearm so that your palm faces the net. This will turn the racket face and make it also face the net and let you hit the ball squarely on the nose, the proper place for a flat shot. The turning action of the forearm also helps increase racket speed, and since flat serves are usually intended to be fast serves, you should use this action to supplement arm extension and wrist flexion. In order to minimize the amount of spin, swing your racket straight into the ball along the intended line of flight, rather than across the line as in spin serves.

PLACING THE SERVE

In advanced play, accuracy as well as speed is an asset when serving. You should be able to hit wide to the receiver's right or left, or straight at him if necessary. In addition, you should be able to vary the kind of spin on the ball to accompany each of the different placements. For example, a slice with a great deal of sidespin is best used to serve wide to the receiver's right. Top spin, when combined with sidespin, can be used effectively when aiming to the receiver's left, and flat serves can be used effectively for all three placements.

Though many players prefer to change the placement of the toss for each different kind of serve, it isn't necessary to do so. You should try to toss consistently to one spot and make subtle changes in the position of your wrist and hand to place the racket properly on the ball. For a flat shot, meet the ball on the nose and swing straight along the intended line of flight. For a basic spin serve, meet the ball on the nose while curling your wrist to brush the racket across the left eye. For a slice, meet the ball on the left cheek while the racket moves along a line toward the center of the service court. The ball will then have sidespin as if rotating on a vertical axis and will curve to the left. In addition, the curve will cause the ball to bounce to the left, to the receiver's forehand side. The slice generally is used to force the receiver wide when serving from the deuce court.

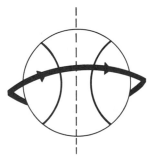

Fig. 3.7 On a slice serve, the ball is struck a glancing blow on the left cheek of the imaginary face. As a result the ball has sidespin and rotates on an imaginary vertical axis as shown.

FOOTWORK WHEN SERVING

Rotation of the trunk is an important point of form when serving. When you do it properly and combine it with a shift of weight, your right side will move

Do you have a clear mental picture of the differences in racket contact with the ball required to produce a flat serve, a slice, a top spin, or a combination of top spin and sidespin?

counterclockwise across the baseline as you swing. The extent to which you bring your right side around with force determines the amount of force in your swing to a large extent. Here, footwork is a matter to consider.

There are several variations on footwork that can increase the power of your swing. You may simply step across the line with your right foot after contact, as if this were a natural outcome of your swing. Or you may jump upward and across the line to land on your right foot; your counterclockwise body turn then becomes part pivot and part jump, which drives your right hip and shoulder around with more force than when you merely step across the line. The upward thrust combined with body rotation creates a sort of rising spiral effect much like a figure skater executing a leaping spin. It may help if you practice with that analogy in mind.

Another method has become popular among top-flight players, and it may work well for you. As you swing, jump upward and forward, but do not cross your right foot over your left. Instead, let it trail behind slightly, and land on your left foot. Emphasize the upward thrust here, rather than the body rotation. The hitting motion is actually an upward motion (from the back-scratching position to the ball) so that you may be able to gain racket speed by jumping upward.

The question of which of these methods to use is best answered from a practical standpoint. Since all three kinds of foot movements are workable, all are worth experimenting with. Whichever gives you the best results should be the one you settle on.

ADJUSTING YOUR STANCE AND TOSS

If you are serving for maximum speed, it may help to modify your stance, toss, and swing. Adjust your right foot to make it point toward the right rear corner of your court. As you start your backswing, raise your left heel and point your left foot and knee toward the sideline. You then will be able to turn your upper body clockwise more than you normally do. You can use the potential built up in such a "coiled" position to generate more force in your counterclockwise body turn as you swing. The result is likely to be more racket speed and a faster serve.

This exaggerated body action will complicate your toss somewhat, but that disadvantage may be compensated for by an improved serve. As your hips and shoulders turn clockwise during your backswing, your tossing arm will move naturally in that direction. Consequently you will have to toss the ball forward and upward, instead of straight up. Your arm also must move in that direction to place the ball accurately at the contact point. Imagine that your arm is tracing a large J in the air as you toss.

The butt-in-the-palm grip, the finger action just before contact, and the jump techniques described in preceding sections also may help increase racket speed.

CORRECTING SERVICE FAULTS

Errors in direction can usually be corrected by adjusting the racket's position on the ball. If you hit the ball too far to the left, it is probably because you placed your racket too far over toward the right side of the ball—too close to the left ear of the face on the ball. You should adjust your wrist to place the racket on the left cheek or possibly even the nose.

If, after adjusting the position of the racket on the ball, you still hit too far to the left, you will probably have to change the line of your swing. Swing across the reference line more than you did on your earlier misses.

If you hit the ball into the net, you made contact toward the top of the ball. Adjust the timing of your wrist action so that you can hit the ball on the nose. If, on the other hand, the ball went too far, adjust the wrist action to make contact a bit lower on the face of the ball.

Often, however, bad wrist and racket position results from an inaccurate toss. If you toss too far forward, toward the net, you will almost always hit into the net, and if you throw the ball back too far, you will usually hit it too deep. In these cases you must first correct your toss in order to correct the racket's position on the ball.

All these adjustments in the position of the racket at contact require adjustments in either the position of the wrist, the toss, or both. Herein lies the secret of effective serving: you must make a consistently accurate toss, and you must have a loose wrist and still control your wrist action during the swing. Make whatever corrections are necessary and appropriate after having served a fault on your first try. You are allowed two tries to get one serve in. Use your first miss as a guide from which you learn what to do differently on your second try. Don't simply repeat the same mistake twice in a row; make a correction.

The volleys

4

Volleys generally should be played as offensive shots. Though you may not be able to use them that way now, you should practice to develop that ability. Learn to use your volleys to reach an attacking position at the net and to win with placements when you have gotten there. Playing exclusively from the backcourt may win for you occasionally, but playing an all-court game—good ground strokes, effective serving, and winning volleys—should be your objective. Only when you can combine these will you be a finished player. Only then will you be able to take full advantage of your ground strokes and your knowledge of tactics and strategy. Work on your volleys now, so that they develop at the same rate as your ground strokes and serves.

In your early volley instruction, you were probably taught to hit from the ideal volley location, midway between the net and the service line, and you were probably told to block or punch the ball with very little swing. This technique is only applicable sometimes at higher levels of play, however. There are some changes and variations required now to enable you to react quickly to the faster tempo of play and to hit effectively from various locations in your court. Several such variations are described here. Practice them— they will help turn your uncertain, tentative volleys into effective weapons.

THE GRIP

Perhaps the most important adjustment made in high-level net play is in the grip. The Eastern forehand grip is no longer adequate. Instead, you should now use the Continental grip, the same one recommended for serving. With the Continental, in which your hand is more on the top plane of the handle than on the back plane, you will be able to hit from both the forehand and backhand sides without changing grips. This is a big advantage because in fast play there isn't always time to change.

But even though you do not change grips, you will have to adjust your wrist and elbow to place the racket properly in the hitting positions. On the forehand you will have to cock your wrist and lay it back. You will also have to keep your elbow down in order to have your racket slanted and angled properly at contact. On the backhand you will have to hit with a straight wrist and with your elbow away from your body.

One simple way to see and feel these wrist and elbow adjustments is to stand in your normal ready stance and place the racket at contact points for imaginary forehand and backhand volleys. Do not move your feet or turn sideways. You will see that the wrist and elbow positions you use for a forehand will not be suitable for a backhand. You will also see that on the forehand your laid-back wrist creates an angle between your hand and forearm, while on the backhand your hand is more in line with your forearm. Practice to make these adjustments, even though you do not have to change grips to volley.

THE READY POSITION

Always cradle the racket at the throat with your left hand as you return to the ready position between shots. Use your left hand to keep the racket head up and to help move the racket back during the backswing, especially on the backhand.

Your right hand should do its part in holding the racket head up, too. Cock your wrist while in the ready position for volleys; you will be more ready to hit than you would be if your wrist were loose and relaxed. These minor adjustments may give you a little more quickness and make you a more effective volleyer.

VARIATIONS IN THE SWING

As an elementary player you were shown a simple kind of volley in which you placed your racket at the intended contact point and merely held it there to intercept the ball and block it. You also may have been taught to move your racket toward the ball with a kind of punching action after making only a very slight backswing. All this was good instruction, but the block and punch volleys are only two of several kinds of volleys necessary for advanced play. At times you will have to vary your techniques, depending on your court position, the position of your opponent, and the purpose of your shot. Other kinds of volleys to use in various situations are the drag volley, the snap volley, the drive volley, and the drop volley. Learn when and how to use them.

The Drag Volley

On the drag volley the ball is struck a downward, glancing blow while the racket face is either vertical or slanted skyward. The combination of the swing plane and the racket slant prolongs contact somewhat and thus provides more control than a more direct, solid hit does. Use the drag volley when you want to hit a medium or soft shot with a minimum of risk.

Fig. 4.1   On the forehand volley, the wrist is cocked and laid back to raise the racket above and behind the ball. The wrist leads during the forward swing so that the racket is dragged down and across the ball.

Fig. 4.2   On the backhand drag volley, slight arm action at the shoulder and elbow enables the hitter to drag the racket down and across the ball.

The Snap Volley

When you need more force and speed in your shot than the drag motion provides, use a snap volley. As the name implies, you snap your wrist as you meet the ball. Lay your wrist back during your backswing, then make it straighter as you hit. The quicker your wrist action, the more force you will add to your swing. Grip tightly at impact to make a firm wrist. Since ball speed is your objective, hit the ball flat; make a square, solid hit rather than the glancing hit of a drag volley. On the backhand you can add elbow action by straightening your arm somewhat to supplement wrist action.

The Drive Volley

The drive volley is especially suitable when you want to hit aggressively at a high ball. For this volley you can make a longer backswing and a longer follow-through than in the other kinds of volleys. You can generate racket speed either by arm action alone or by combining arm action with body rotation. Because of the longer swing and your intention to hit hard, there is a greater element of risk in this shot than in other volleys. To reduce the risk, hold your racket firmly. This will eliminate wrist action and reduce elbow action. The result will be a kind of one-piece swing in which your racket appears to be an extension of your forearm.

Fig. 4.3 Judy Tegart Dalton, a world-class Australian, is shown leaping into a drive volley. In this stroke, used to hit aggressively at a high ball, both the backswing and the follow-through are longer, and there is usually more body action than in the other volleys.

The Drop Volley

The drop volley is a drop shot made as a volley and is used for the same purpose as a drop shot. The intention is to hit the volley softly so that the ball barely clears the net and has too little force to be playable by your opponent. When alternated with crisp, deep volleys, it often catches a baseliner by surprise. Expecting a deeper shot, he is not ready to run forward, and as a result he is not always able to reach the ball before it takes its second bounce.

To hit a drop volley accurately, you must take the speed off the oncoming ball. You can do this in either of two ways: (1) by loosening your grip and relaxing your wrist at impact, or (2) by drawing your racket back and away from the ball with a short, quick backward motion of your forearm. Loosening your grip and wrist at impact will cushion the impact between the oncoming ball and your racket. As a result your racket will recoil or "give" a bit as the ball hits it. If you turn your wrist and forearm quickly in a clockwise direction at the same time, you will put backspin on the ball. You should try to hit softly enough and with enough spin to make the ball drop vertically, close to the net, and bounce vertically or at least with very little forward carry after the bounce.

MOVING TO VOLLEY

When you run forward to volley after a serve or an approach shot, stop running and hop to a ready position just as your opponent's racket meets the ball. Jump to a wide stance with your knees bent and your hips low. Don't set yourself into a solid, stationary stance, however; pause only momentarily, then move to play the volley. The procedure by which you stop running to make yourself ready to volley is called "checking," "splitting," or making a split stop. Regardless of how you describe it, you should hop to a ready position in which you feel light and springy. Be ready to spring into action to intercept your opponent's shot.

Your moves from the ready position should vary, depending on the direction of your opponent's shot. If the ball is comfortably alongside of you, you can simply pivot on the foot that is closest to the ball and swing the other foot forward, toward the net, as you hit. On wider balls you will often have to swing that foot across your body and toward the sideline. On the other hand, if the ball is close enough to crowd you, you will have to lean away and step away from the ball with that same foot.

At times you may get caught off balance a bit and be able to reach sideways only with the foot that is closer to the ball. If you can reach the ball this way, that is fine. But do not expect the ball to be hit that close to you. Expect a wide shot, and be prepared to make a crossover step with the foot that is farther from the ball. Crossover steps give you maximum reach on both sides, especially when made from a wide stance.

Balls hit directly at your body can be handled best with your backhand. Simply by moving your elbow to your right, you can place the racket face in

Fig. 4.4 Jim McManus was probably caught off balance for this low forehand volley. Instead of swinging his right foot across and forward, as he would have liked to have done, he simply leaned on his left foot and reached out to meet the ball. Even top-flight players have to improvise. Often, they settle for getting the ball back, regardless of form. (See chapter? for illustrations of conventional footwork on volleys.)

front of your belt buckle or your chest. A slight backward and forward motion with your elbow will let you get enough force into your swing, though this will only be a defensive shot. It's a useful play, however; remember that you can protect your body with a backhand.

If your serve or approach shot is good enough to draw a weak return that floats softly to you, move forward to play it after making your split stop. Moving forward to play the ball higher in its flight and from a position closer to the net will let you play the shot more aggressively. Remember, the split stop should be only a momentary pause. Do not wait for the ball to come to you; move sideways to intercept or forward to hit it sooner.

The length of your swing depends on your position in the court and on your intentions. If you are hitting from the ideal volley position, midway between the net and the service line, you will not need much backswing or follow-through. But when you are hitting from near your service line, your swing may have to be a little longer in order to get depth on your shot. However, if you are trying to place your shot at an opposing net man's feet, as you often must do in doubles, you must shorten your swing even from this position.

PLACING YOUR VOLLEYS

In an ideal situation the technique for placing your volleys can be identical to that used on ground strokes. To hit angled shots, meet the ball either sooner or later than your point of contact for straight-ahead shots. You will not always be able to get into the ideal position for net shots, however; the ball will not always be comfortably within your reach and you will not always have time to move as you would like. Consequently, you will not always be able to make the fine adjustments in timing needed for accurate placement. In such cases, you must change your volleying form slightly to get the kind of hit you want.

On the forehand, for example, you should make adjustments in your wrist position at contact. By bending the wrist either more or less than you do for straight-ahead shots, you can vary the direction of your hit. To hit to your right, bend your wrist back and make contact on the near side of the ball. To hit to your left, straighten your wrist and make contact on the far side of the ball. To hit straight ahead, adjust your wrist somewhere between the two positions you used on angled shots.

On the backhand you must adjust the position of your elbow to vary the direction of your shots. To hit to your left, move your elbow forward, toward the net, so that it leads the swing at contact. To hit to your right, keep your elbow close to your body to permit your racket head to lead a bit at contact. For straight-ahead shots, keep your elbow somewhere between those two positions.

With practice you will learn to make these adjustments quickly. Practice until these moves become habitual, and remember: to place your forehand volleys, make adjustments with your wrist; to place backhands, adjust your elbow.

Footwork on ground strokes

5

Good footwork entails more than simply getting to the ball and returning to good position after a shot. It includes moving into position in a way that enables you to take an efficient hitting stance, even under difficult conditions. An efficient stance is sometimes "open," sometimes "closed." At times the hitter is perfectly balanced as he swings. At other times he is off balance, but in a controlled way. Good movers make adjustments in their steps—they adjust the size, the speed, and the timing—so they can take whichever stance is best or possible on each hit. This requires speed of foot, agility, mobility, body control, and balance.

MOVING TO HIT

For baseline play, try to be in a ready stance one step behind the center mark as your opponent meets the ball. This will put you in the best position to move in the various directions required in play. To reach balls eight or ten feet to your side, you may have to turn sideways and run to the ball. You can begin your run with either foot, but try to get set to hit with your body weight on your right foot (in the case of a forehand). This lets you step in with the left foot as you swing. Move with little steps because you will be able to adjust them better and because they give more starting speed than big ones do. Start your backswing as soon as you begin to move, and adjust it with reference to the amount of time you have to make it.

If you have to hurry to reach a wide ball, one wider than the sideline, the "gravity method," in which you use the force of gravity to get in motion, may be your best method. To use this, simultaneously turn sideways toward the oncoming ball and lift the foot that is closest to the ball. With such an action you will start to fall in the direction you want to run. To keep from falling, place that foot alongside the other foot. Then, quickly step toward the sideline, and continue running to intercept the ball. Your second step here (with your left foot if you are running for a forehand) should be no longer than

Fig. 5.1 A baseliner hurries toward his right sideline to return a shot from his opponent. Here he has too little time to set himself into the sideways position for his backswing. Good control of his body weight, however, enables him to shift his weight to his left foot slightly before contact. Unable to stop before hitting, he is forced into making a recovery step with his right foot after contact. This kind of footwork and body control is often necessary in advanced play.

to the point under your center of gravity so that it won't block or slow your movement.

If you have to move only five or six feet to reach a ball, the most convenient way may be to skip or shuffle to it. To move to your right, simply push off with your left foot, while raising the other and moving it to the right several inches. Place your weight on the right foot and bring the left up alongside it. A quick shift of weight to your left foot will permit another pushoff and another skip to the right. After your second skip, pivot on your right foot and swing your left foot across to place your body in a hitting position.

Fig. 5.2 The author helps a student in his first attempts to learn the gravity method of moving. Here he supports the student until he learns to place his feet properly. In play the player will fall to his right as he lifts his right foot. He will use the force of gravity then to get in motion and will place his right foot alongside the left and step with the left as he runs to intercept the ball.

Skip only when two skips will let you reach the ball. Three or more skips are awkward and slow. If you skipped to the ball, you can skip back to position, but if you ran to the ball, you will probably have to run back.

Moving toward the rear fence can be done in much the same way. If two skips will get you into position, you can move that way. Start by pivoting on your left foot and at the same time swinging your right foot backwards. Then skip toward the rear fence.

On fast, deep balls you will probably have to turn and run to get into position. Start by drawing your right foot back and then crossing your left foot over your right. Run sideways toward the rear fence. While running, look toward the net at the ball. Go back far enough to let high-bouncing balls come down into your "strike zone," where you can handle them conveniently,

Have you practiced the several footwork patterns that are used most often?
Do you know when to run for the ball rather than skip? What are two effective ways to stop before hitting?

and to let fast, deep balls come up to waist height, where you can handle them
comfortably.

To get away from a close ball, move your right foot back and to your left
while making your backswing. Then, step toward the left net post with the
left foot as you make your forward swing. For balance, drag your right foot
toward your left during the swing.

Moving forward to hit is easy. Simply walk or run toward the spot at
which you intend to meet the ball. You can start moving with either foot,
but adjust your steps so that you can get set to hit with your weight on your
right foot. Make the final step with your left foot, swinging as you step.

To return to the waiting position, you can run to within a step or so of
the center mark, then jump and face the net as you land in the ready position. Or you can turn sooner—when you get to within five or six feet of the
mark—and cover the remaining distance by skipping. Both methods are good;
the first is faster, however, and should be used when you are pressed for time.

When you run to reach a wide ball, start moving quickly and try to get
to the ball in time to get into a balanced hitting stance. Hurry to the ball,
and then, if there is time, slow down as you swing. Try not to hit while
moving. As you approach the ball, plant the foot that is closer to the net as
you start your forward swing. Use this step to reduce sideways movement. Try
not to hit with that foot in air in the middle of a step.

When you need a quick start, use little steps. You can accelerate each
time you put a foot down. Lengthen your strides only when you have gained
speed.

Supplementary shots

6

The forehand and backhand drives, the serve, and the volleys are the basic shots of tennis. But they are not all that is needed to play effectively at the intermediate and advanced levels. Several other strokes must be learned to permit you to play well whether you rely on backcourt defensive play or on aggressive net play. A description of each of these follows. Work on them at the same time that you work on the basic shots. Failure to develop them at the same rate as the basics will make you a "warped" player with weaknesses and deficiencies that are certain to be exploited by your opponents. Practice these supplementary shots; make them part of your arsenal now.

THE LOB

The lob usually is played as a defensive shot against a net man who has made a good attack or has a weak overhead smash. It is commonly used to draw an error on a missed smash or to allow time for recovery into good position. The lobber intends to return the smash with a drive to the smasher's feet. Occasionally, however, the lob is meant to clear the net man completely and bounce for an outright winner. Such a shot—usually called an offensive lob—carries a great deal of top spin and so is hit with a full swing and a vigorous brushing motion. It is truly an advanced stroke and should not be attempted until the simpler defensive lob is learned.

To make full use of the defensive lob, you must be able to lob with either of two different kinds of swings, one of which resembles your ground stroke. If you are returning a drive or a volley, try to make your lob motion look exactly like your drive motion. The more deception you employ, the more likely you are to succeed in drawing a weak return. However, since your intention is to loft the ball more than you do on drives, your forward swing must be more upward than it is for drives. At contact, turn your forearm back a bit to permit you to hit under the ball. Keep your grip and wrist firm, and lift and carry the ball forward and upward with an open racket face. This

Fig. 6.1 The upward slant of the racket is shown clearly in this photo of a player making a backhand lob. The forward swing was started slightly below the height of contact, and the racket was swung upward into the ball.

will impart some backspin and permit greater control than a flat shot. Keep the racket in contact with the ball as long as you can, and steer the ball, guiding it upward as you follow through.

When lobbing a fast ball that has been served or smashed at you, you will not have time for a full swing, nor will you need one. Instead, your lob motion should resemble that of your volley. But, of course, your intention is to hit up, and so you must move the racket in an upward plane rather than in a downward one as you would on a volley. Bend your wrist back and meet the ball in front of you. To take speed off the oncoming ball, put backspin on your shot by turning your racket under the ball at contact.

The offensive top-spin lob, meant to barely clear the volleyer's reach and bounce away for a winner, is used much less frequently in match play than the defensive lob, and it is successful less frequently, too. Even top players use it almost exclusively on the forehand—few can manage the wrist control and wrist action needed for consistent control on the backhand. It is useful as a surprise shot against a net man, however, and you should be familiar with it and practice it on your forehand after you have learned to use the defensive lob.

In practice it may help if you think of this shot as a very high, looping, top-spin drive. Start your forward swing lower than you normally do, and swing in more of an upward plane. As you brush the racket along the back of the ball, try to carry the ball up on the strings. Finish high—higher than you do on drives—and use your upward follow-through to lift the ball up.

The lob volley is played exactly like the other "touch" volleys described earlier, except that the racket is beveled back more to provide the additional loft and spin needed for control. It is an extremely delicate shot and must, therefore, be played with a short stroke and firm wrist. It is used in both

How do offensive and defensive lobs differ in their trajectory? If you hope to force a poor return from your opponent, to which side will you usually send a lob volley? When should you play a lob on the fly instead of letting it bounce?

singles and doubles for both offensive and defensive purposes. The intention is to catch the opponent by surprise during a volley exchange. The ball is meant to clear the opponent's reach completely or to draw a weak return that can be volleyed away for a winner. For this latter purpose the lob volley is usually played to an opponent's backhand side.

THE OVERHEAD SMASH

Regardless of how quickly you move or how well you volley, you will not get full value from your net game if you cannot handle lobs well. Smart opponents will soon discover your weakness. To prevent them from using lobs and lessening the effectiveness of your net game, you must develop your smash at the same rate at which you learn to volley. Practice the two together at every training session.

The swing on the overhead comes rather naturally after the serve has been learned. It is very much like the serve, though there is one major difference between the two swings. Fortunately, the difference is not a matter of complicating the serve swing but rather of simplifying it. Almost all good smashers, even those who have a long, full windup on the serve, shorten the swing for a smash. Rather than letting the racket drop down past the knee in the windup, they carry it back higher, often past the right ear, to get it into the hitting position. This more direct backswing makes movement and timing easier; it is strongly recommended for your use.

Use the same grip here that you use when serving. Reach up and forward to contact the ball in front of you. During your swing, adjust your wrist position so you can meet the ball with an open racket face. Hit the ball as flatly as you can; do not deliberately put sidespin or overspin on it.

The ideal hitting stance is sideways, much like your serving stance. Make your backswing as you move into your stance from the ready position. Try to get set under the line of flight of the ball. Hold your racket up behind you, cocked and ready to swing. As you swing, step toward the net.

The forward swing is upward. Reach up to meet the ball; do not stoop or bend your knees to hit. Start your swing with your racket up and behind you and with your body weight on your rear foot. Make a quick wrist and elbow motion to dip the racket down behind your shoulders, then swing it up and forward to the point of contact. Try to meet the ball when your arm is fully extended. For maximum power, use a lot of wrist action; for less power, use less wrist. Follow through along the intended line of flight of the ball.

Ideally, you should try to be in such a position that at contact the ball will be where you would have thrown it had you been permitted to serve from

Fig. 6.2   An overhead smash. Note the high backswing, the skip steps to move into position, and the swing up and over the ball.

that spot. Your position relative to the ball at contact will vary, therefore, depending on your distance from the net. If you are very close to the net, you can meet the ball while it is well in front of you. If you are back as far as the service line, you will have to meet it later.

On many smashes, however, you will not have time to get into the ideal position under the ball. At times, the ball will be either farther in front or in back of you at contact than you would like it to be. You must make adjustments with your arm and wrist to give you the proper racket angle on the ball.

If you judge the ball to be short (in front of you), turn to your right and move your left foot forward, taking the racket back as you turn. Move forward to get under the ball by taking little shuffle steps, keeping the left foot closer to the net. Time and adjust your steps so that you will be able to make the last step with the left foot as you start your forward swing.

On a deeper lob that causes you to go back, turn and move your right foot back. Take the racket back as you turn. Move backward to get under the ball by taking little shuffle steps, keeping your left foot close to the net. Time your moves and adjust your steps to enable you to swing and step in with your left foot when the ball is within your reach.

Occasionally, your opponent will succeed in getting a lob so far over you that you will not be able to stop, get set, and step in as you swing. Instead, you will have to jump backward to reach the ball. This is an exciting play and always appeals to spectators. Fortunately, it is not as difficult as it appears.

As you move back, time your steps so that you can push off the rear foot as you swing. Jump and make a "scissors" kick by swinging the right foot forward and the left one back. Land on the left foot after you make contact with the ball. Quickly regain your balance, and move forward or backward to get into position for your opponent's next shot.

Very high lobs are often difficult to time and judge. Let them bounce, then hit them exactly as you would if the ball were in flight. Very high lobs drop nearly vertically and, thus, bounce nearly vertically. As a result, you will not have to back up much farther to play them after the bounce than if you had played them on the fly. The advantage you then gain in easier judgment and timing will offset the disadvantage of giving up a few feet of court position. But if you find that after letting a lob bounce you have to retreat five or six steps to play it, you made a mistake in judgment; you should not have let it bounce.

Judging the flight of the ball is one of the most difficult things for inexperienced players to master. Even among top players, the ability to do so sometimes varies from day to day as conditions of play vary. Wind, of course, makes the flight of the ball erratic; a bright sun can be very bothersome, and a deep blue sky often causes errors in depth perception. Under any of these conditions, it may be wise to let the ball bounce in order to get a safer play on it. At times like these, many good players point the fingers of the left hand at the ball as they move into position to hit. They feel this helps them concentrate on the ball, wtach it closely, and make a more accurate judgment of its speed, position, and trajectory. This trick may work for you; try it.

THE HALF VOLLEY

The half volley, the little pickup shot made on a "short hop," is really not a volley at all. It is more like a ground stroke because the ball first hits the ground and then is stroked. The racket meets the ball a split second after it has bounced and started to rise. The big difference between it and a drive is in the length of the swing. The swing should be shorter and more controlled than that of a full-length drive because you seldom need as much length in your shot. You are hitting from closer to the net and hitting at a very low ball; consequently, the shot must be played more carefully and with more restraint than a full-length drive.

The half volley is usually played as a defensive shot and used only when necessary on low returns. This often occurs immediately after an approach shot. The net rusher does not always have time to move into the ideal volley position; he often has to play his first net shot from the service line, and from there, he often has to play a ball at his feet. Immediately after the hit, experienced net men move up to the ideal position where they are less likely to have to play a half volley on the next shot.

The logical grip to use is the volley grip because you make this shot from a volley position. Turn sideways if you can, and use the crossover steps described earlier to reach the ball. Bend your knees enough so that you can lower the racket head to the ball without having to change your wrist angle much from its low volley position. Watch the ball carefully and "nurse" it up and over as carefully as you do on low volleys.

Direction and control are attained by adjusting the slant of the hitting surface. If you are hitting from very close to the net, your racket face must be open more than it should be when hitting from farther back. Wrist and elbow adjustments are often needed to adjust the racket. As you swing, keep a firm grip and wrist. Swing smoothly through the contact point and keep the racket in contact with the ball as long as you can.

THE DROP SHOT AND DROP VOLLEY

The drop shot is a soft, delicate shot used against an opponent who is in the backcourt. It is a "touch" shot requiring precise timing and delicate racket control. Sometimes it is meant to win the point outright against a slow opponent (especially on slow courts), but it is also used both to tire an opponent by causing him to run and to bring him up to the net when his net play is weaker than his backcourt play.

The intention is to make the ball barely clear the net while it is dropping nearly vertically so that it will have very little "carry" on the bounce. The swing should resemble a ground stroke drive until just before contact. Then,

---

In comparison with the drive, is the half volley more or less forceful? Is the grip the same? Does the ball bounce closer to the feet?

---

as you bring your racket forward into the ball, turn your wrist sharply to open the racket face. This lets you hit under the ball and apply backspin to it while at the same time giving it the lift it needs to clear the net. Precisely at contact, relax your grip and wrist to deaden the impact; this is how to get the softness and touch needed.

The drop volley (a drop shot made from a volley) is used to supplement crisp volleys. It is used for the same purposes and in much the same way as a drop shot. Here, however, you are in a volley position, so your grip, stance, and swing resemble the volley rather than the ground stroke. Disguise this shot by making it look like a crisp volley, but here, too, turn your wrist at contact, loosen your grip, and hit under the ball to give it backspin. Try to make it drop vertically, close to the net, with enough backspin to cause it to bounce vertically or to at least reduce the forward carry after the bounce.

THE SLICE

The slice is a supplementary stroke to the drive, made from both the forehand and backhand sides. It can be used effectively for defensive purposes, as an attacking shot, and as a general rally shot, particularly on the backhand.

Strike the ball with a downward blow, keeping an open racket face to put backspin on the ball. The greater the downward path and slant of the racket, the more spin will be produced. These two variables—racket path and racket angle—produce varying amounts of spin. Many top players are able to make these adjustments at will and use the shot to vary the pace and spin for purposes of upsetting an opponent's rhythm and timing. Generally, however, the spin is applied for the purpose of maintaining control off the racket, rather than for influencing the bounce of the ball.

You can use the slice as a defensive shot when you have been forced wide in your court. Hit it with only moderate speed to slow the tempo of the rally and to get time to recover to good position. You also can use it as a defense against hard serves coming in close to your body on the backhand. On these your body often will get in the way of your backswing. Consequently, you must swing across your body to generate enough racket speed to make a good return.

The slice backhand is the most effective way to return high-bouncing serves, such as the American twist. For these serves, play the ball early from up inside your baseline. Play the ball on the rise as it comes up above waist level. Use a short swing and adjust the plane of your swing and the slant of your racket to enable you to pull the rising ball down. Aim at the service line; try to make your opponent hit upward defensively, so that you can pass him more easily on your next shot.

The backhand slice often can be used as an approach shot during a baseline rally. You should hit the ball slowly enough so that you have time to

Fig. 6.3   A backhand slice. The racket face is slanted skyward slightly and is moved forward and downward into the ball, thus imparting backspin.

move up to a good volley position. Use it cautiously, however; either place your shot very deep or angle it sharply to force your opponent into trying a difficult passing shot.

You also can attack with this stroke on your forehand by making only a slight adjustment in your swing. Change the path of your forward swing to make the racket travel across the ball from right to left (swing from the outside in) as it brushes down its back side. Aim down the line to your opponent's backhand and try to curve the ball a bit in that direction. Its slow flight and low bounce away from him (resulting from the spin on the ball) will give you time to move up to a good volley position and give him a difficult low shot to play.

Most frequently the slice is used as a rally shot, particularly on the backhand, because most players have less confidence in their ability to sustain rallies with drives. It is used to maneuver the opponent or at least play him evenly while waiting for a chance to attack. Learn to use it for this purpose.

Fig. 6.4   A forehand slice used as a running approach shot. The racket is moved forward, downward, and across the ball to impart backspin and side-spin. The combination of spins causes the ball to curve in flight and to bounce low to the receiver's left.

THE RUNNING APPROACH SHOT

If you do not volley and serve well enough to play "the big game," or if the court surface is too slow to permit those kinds of tactics, you will have to rely on your ground strokes to pave the way for a safe approach to the volley position. You will have to maneuver your opponent with deep or angled drives, after which you can attack his weakness and move in to volley. For consistent effectiveness, however, the approach to the net must be planned carefully. Generally, you should not go up to the net unless you are hitting a strong shot from from on or inside your baseline, when you can hit deep to your opponent's weak stroke or to where he is weak in position.

Your opponent also will be trying to keep his returns deep to prevent you from moving in. This means you have to learn to take the ball "early," on the bounce or on the rise if necessary. You may have to hit while on the move

---

Can you explain why the backhand slice is effective in controlling the American twist serve? Have you practiced using the backhand slice to give you a chance to get into volley position?

---

and while facing the net. But this does not necessarily place you at a disadvantage. Hitting on the move gives you a quicker start to the volley position, and the facing-the-net stance gives you good weight control and balance.

To make such a running approach shot, step toward the ball with your near foot (the right foot on a forehand, for example) and make your backswing as you step. Place that foot naturally, with the toes pointing toward the net post. Start your forward swing as you step toward the net with your left foot. Time your swing so that contact occurs before the transfer of weight is completed—before the left foot comes in contact with the ground.

Fig. 6.5 A forehand drive used as a running approach shot. The player steps toward the ball with his right foot and hits while his left foot is in the air. The upward swing plane imparts top spin.

If the oncoming ball is slow enough to let you move forward more than just one step, move close enough to the ball so that you face the net as you swing, while stepping toward the net with the left foot.

Whether you have time for only one step or can move in farther to hit, do not cross the left foot over and wait for the ball to come to you. Step toward the ball with your right foot. This will give you a running start and let you hit from a full step closer to the net.

This method of moving in to a shot can be used effectively following a service return to the net, a situation you often will encounter in doubles.

Singles strategy

7

There is no question that a strong serve is an asset in top-flight competition. When placed accurately with adequate speed, it often draws weak returns that can be volleyed away for winners. This style of play in which the server runs forward to volley is known as "the big game." The idea is to attack at the first opportunity, to put pressure on the opponent even when serving.

Although the serve-and-volley game is often the winning way in fast tournament play, it may not be right for you. You may not be able to rely on cannonball serves and slashing volleys to win. If you do not develop the ability to make these shots consistently, even under pressure—and this may take more time and effort than you are willing to give—you will be tougher to beat and have more fun at the game by using a style of play built around your own physical equipment and mental qualities.

PLAYING AN ALL-AROUND GAME

Much of your early instruction and practice time was spent on ground strokes; you rallied from the backcourt and learned to keep the ball in play and control its direction. Your best plan now is to develop these ground strokes to the point where you can use them as the basis for an "all-around game." Consistent returns of serves, deep baseline drives, accurate passing shots, and forcing approach shots—these can win for you now, even without a cannonball serve.

If, for example, you are slow to react and you can't serve hard or accurately enough, you would be foolish to follow every serve in to the volley position. Instead, you would be smart to wait for a safer chance to go in to the net. Stay back after your serve and rally with your opponent until he misses or gives you a short shot. When it comes, move in quickly to get it high on the bounce if possible, and hit a deep approach shot to his weak stroke or to where he is weak in position.

This safe chance to go to the net doesn't come along very often in the normal course of events. Usually, you will have to create it by maneuvering your opponent, making him use his weaker stroke so that he makes a short shot. This means you must be able to play steady tennis, avoiding errors and not giving your opponent a chance to attack. In other words, you must be able to sustain the rally.

At all except top levels of play, rally shots should be hit to your opponent's backhand because that is usually his weaker stroke. Since he also will play to your weaker stroke, the rally will become a series of backhand crosscourt shots. In advanced tournament play the idea of hitting consistently to an opponent's backhand isn't carried out quite so strictly. Few ranking players have difficulty maintaining baseline rallies with their backhands. For this reason tournament players mix crosscourts with down-the-line shots in an attempt to create an opening or a weakness by moving their opponent. But until you graduate into the tournament players' class, your opponents will have a built-in weakness, and it will usually be their backhand. Logically then, most of your rally and attacking shots should be hit to that weakness.

CONTROLLING THE RALLY

The deep backhand crosscourt is the basic shot in baseline tennis. When you have developed confidence in your ability to make it consistently, even under the pressure of crucial points, you will have taken the first step toward developing the temperament needed for tournament play.

As you gain experience, you will learn to use the shot more advantageously than for simply keeping the ball in play. Subtle changes in depth, speed, and placement will enable you to control rallies and maneuver to get the first chance to attack. In backcourt play, the player who controls the rally and then decides wisely how to end it is usually the winner.

For half of match play, controlling the rally begins with an effective serve. Even if you can't serve aces as the Davis Cup players do, you should use your serve as an offensive shot to get a good, solid first blow in to your opponent. Try to put him on the defensive immediately, even though you don't intend to follow your serve in to volley. Place most of your serves to his weaker stroke—his backhand—to keep him from attacking with his returns, but serve often enough to his forehand to keep him centered. Don't let him move over to cover his backhand. If you can control your serve well enough, serve straight in to him occasionally to crowd him and keep him guessing.

When returning the serve, your first objective should be to prevent your opponent from controlling the rally. Therefore, your first return should be deep enough to keep him from attacking. Normally, after serving he will take a ready position on the baseline, hoping to be able to rally with you and attack you from there. Don't let him. Make him go backwards to hit a backhand for his first shot. If you can do that, you will have succeeded in taking the "sting" out of his serve and will have come out at least even with him rather than on the defensive. In fact, even if you only place a medium-paced shot deep to his backhand, you will have begun already to control the rally.

Although deep shots should be the foundation of your backcourt play, a wise mixture of short, angled shots and deeper ones often will keep your opponent on the run and let you control the rally. Varying the depth of your shots is especially effective if you first have moved him wide and deep on his forehand. A soft shot, preferably a slice, angled short to his backhand will often force him to use his weak stroke while running. Furthermore, he may be lured up to the volley position after this weak shot or even be caught in dangerous "no-man's-land" if he attempts to return to the baseline.

As an alternative plan of attack, try driving or slicing a short, angled shot to your opponent's forehand and then driving or slicing deep to his backhand corner. Even if he normally has a strong backhand, it could lose its effectiveness if he is forced to run diagonally toward his baseline to use it. Intercepting his return with a volley may be easier and more effective when he has run to make the shot than when he can make his return from a set position.

A third strategic plan could begin with a slice short and wide to your opponent's backhand, followed by a deep return to his forehand. If your opponent has to hit while he is off balance and retreating, he is likely to hit less effectively, even if his forehand is normally a strong shot. If his return is short, it doesn't matter whether the ball was hit hard or softly; you can reply effectively with a dropshot designed to land close to the net along your right sideline.

The sequence of shots described in the first of these three plans is the safest. In the other plans, if your first shot—the short angle—is not placed accurately, your opponent may be able to attack with an approach shot to

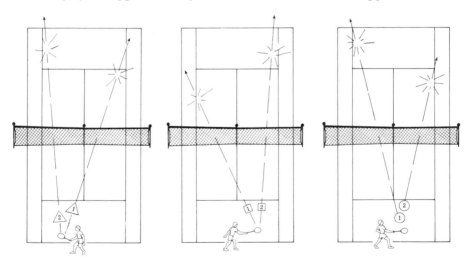

Fig. 7.1   Sketch shows three sequences to use when hitting from the backcourt. Hit deep to your opponent's forehand 1, then short to his backhand 2; or hit short to his forehand 1, then deep to his backhand 2; or finally, hit short and wide to his backhand 1, then follow with a deep shot to his forehand 2.

In each sequence, your third shot will depend on the kind of return your opponent makes. You may advance to the net to volley, you may continue to rally to force him to run, or you may use a dropshot to end the rally.

Choose one of the plans given on pages 52 and 53 for preventing the server from controlling the rally. How many times can you make it work in a practice set?

---

your backhand. In the first plan, however, he is not likely to play so aggressively since he must retrieve a wide, low backhand.

Because you cannot predict your opponent's shots, your sequence may not always develop as planned, but the general idea of mixing short and deep shots is often usable regardless of the placement of his shots. Regardless of which sequence you use, your third shot will often bother your opponent, too, if it is placed behind him as he hurries to recover to good position. This tactic, called "wrong-footing" an opponent, is especially effective on slippery courts such as clay, dirt, and various composition surfaces such as Har Tru, Teniko, and En-Tout-Cas.

HITTING ON THE RISE

In baseline play, a player's ability to return to good position often is related to the amount of time he has between shots. For example, if you have moved your opponent out of the court but you play his return after a long bounce from a position deep behind your baseline, you will give him time to recover for your next shot. Often, to take advantage of his bad position you will have to hit the ball earlier, from a position closer to your baseline. As a beginner, you were probably taught to stay back from the line in order to hit a descending ball. Then you needed time to move into position and to make the stroke properly. Now, however, you must play the ball sooner. It will be greatly to your advantage to be able to hit it while it is rising, for the sooner you hit it, the sooner it will be on its way to your opponent, and the less time he'll have to recover to a good position to chase it down.

As its name implies, in the center theory a player drives or slices to the center of his opponent's court then advances to the net to intercept his returns with volleys. Hitting on the rise may enable you to use this theory as a means of attacking and winning with volleys, because you often will be hitting from inside your baseline and thus have less distance to cover to reach the close-in volley position that it requires.

The advantage of using such a tactic is that the size of the angles your opponent has for passing you is greatly reduced. Indeed, unless your opponent has sharply dropping top-spin shots, it may be extremely difficult for him to hit past you, especially if he is hitting from behind his baseline.

The most effective way to apply this theory is to hit wide to your opponent's forehand and then move in to play your return early enough to force him into hitting his backhand from the center. Very few players can pass easily in such a situation, so you should be prepared for a lob. At the same time, however, you should be ready to move forward after your split stop in case he does try to pass; attempt to intercept his return sooner and higher.

At the same time that the center theory reduces your opponent's angles, it also reduces the size of the angles you have for placing your volleys. Since your opponent is hitting from the center, he is not far from your volleys in any direction, so your volleys must be accurate and forceful to win. You must appraise every aspect of the situation, therefore, before using the center theory. If you can volley better from the center than your opponent can pass from that location, it may be to your advantage to incorporate it into your attack.

CONTROLLING THE DEPTH OF YOUR SHOT

The respective values of both deep and short shots already have been pointed out: deep shots keep the opponent back away from an attacking position; short, angled shots move him and lure him into bad position. To control the depth of your shots, you must control the height at which your balls clear the net. The height at which you hit must vary depending on the speed and

Fig. 7.2 A target board attached to the net may help you learn to control the depth of your shots. You should aim passing shots at the first level, attempting to barely clear the net. Rally shots should be higher, to the second or third levels, to provide a margin of safety and to increase their distance.

purpose of your shot and on your position when you are hitting. Short shots, meant to draw your opponent up into the court, should clear the net by only a foot or two. Other shots, intended for depth, should be higher. Most rally shots should clear the net by two or three feet to provide the depth necessary to keep your opponent behind his baseline.

PLAYING AGAINST A NET MAN

Good ground strokes are needed to combat an opponent's net-rushing tactics. Deep rally shots often cause an opponent to lose patience (one of the qualities needed for good baseline play) and approach the net from deep in the court, sometimes even on a weaker stroke. Such approaches are likely to be less effective than those made on his strong stroke from inside his baseline. If you succeed in luring him into these unsound tactics, you will minimize the effectiveness of his net attack.

When your opponent is in the volleying position, you do not always need to try to pass him outright with a one-shot winner. If his approach is short, you might be able to pass him on your first attempt. But if his approach is good—deep and to your weak stroke—a medium-speed drive or even a slice, placed low to make him hit up, might be a smarter play. You are likely to get another, possibly safer chance to pass.

After making a low shot that your opponent has to volley up or even half volley, be alert for a short, weak return. Move in a step or two to be ready for such a shot; hurry in to get it high on the bounce so you will not have to hit up to him on your next shot.

PLAYING THE POWER GAME

Despite the emphasis here on baseline play—on steadiness and control—you soon may develop a serve strong enough to permit you to play a power game. If you serve well enough to draw weak returns, you certainly should follow your serves in to volley. But you must understand good position play to make the most of your power.

The ideal volley position with respect to distance from the net is about midway between the net and the service line. You will not always be able to reach that position for your first volley, however. Usually you will be forced to hit from a little farther back and then move up to the ideal spot for your next hit. Rather than making a mad dash to the ideal position, you probably will have to move up by degrees, stopping to get ready as your opponent meets the ball, then moving up again after your hit. You should stop only long enough to determine what your opponent intends to do (he may drive hard or slice softly to either your right or left, or he may lob over you). From your "check" position, you will be able to move to meet such returns.

After a hard first serve, you may have time for only two or three steps before your opponent makes his hit. Determine where you are (it will very likely be in "no-man's-land," but you can risk being caught there after a strong serve); make your volley; then move up to a better position for your second shot.

After a softer second serve, you will have more running time, perhaps enough time for four or five steps. These steps will get you up to the service line before you have to pause to play his return. It will take only another step or two to get to the ideal volley position for your second hit.

The proper volley position with respect to the sidelines is midway between the angles of your opponent's possible returns (you should bisect the angle). If he is near an alley, you should be off center to that same side. If he moves over toward the other alley for his next shot, you also must move in that direction. When you are running up for your first volley, run in the direction that puts you closest to the ideal position and on the line of good position just as your opponent hits the ball. This is a matter of judgment—you should select the shortest route to the best volley position. With experience, your judgment will improve and you will guess more accurately.

PLAYING BACKCOURT TENNIS

If neither your serves nor your ground strokes are strong enough to permit you to advance safely to the net, if you cannot move as quickly as net play requires, or if you simply cannot volley well enough to feel confident at the net, your best plan may be to remain in the backcourt and try to win from there. Until you develop the skills and qualities necessary for effective net play, let your ground strokes win for you.

When your plan is to play from the backcourt, there are several factors to consider. Your opponent also may feel that his strength is in his ground strokes, in which case he will stay back and try to outsteady you. Since he is a baseliner by choice, he is probably weak at the net. Therefore, you should try to draw him in and away from his favorite baseline position. Hit a lot of short balls, preferably angled, to his weak stroke or to a weakness in his position. Whenever you are up far enough in your court, use your dropshot to force him to make a low retrieve. Particularly on slow courts and when hitting against a strong wind, short angles and dropshots can be very effective in breaking up an opponent's baseline game.

If he, too, stays at the baseline, his plan is probably to beat you by causing you to overhit, to force you to hit recklessly and carelessly until you miss more shots than you make. Don't let him trick you into these errors! Baseline play is a battle of temperaments as well as strokes. Be patient; play carefully and thoughtfully. Try to detect a weakness in his game. He may not like high backhands, he may hit wildly on running forehands, or he may be lured into hitting down-the-line shots which let you hit crosscourt and keep him running. Quite possibly you can draw errors or weak shots by mixing these shots.

When your opponent does hit short, move in to attack. Even if your net game is relatively weak, you may be able to play well enough to win there if you make strong approach shots. Above all, don't lose patience and go up to volley behind a bad approach shot. After all, you are letting your opponent play from his favorite position; make certain that your attack is strong enough to offset his advantage.

When you, as a baseliner, find yourself opposing a net rusher, your problems are quite different. You must be able to pass him or make him miss on his volleys and smashes more often than you miss on your drives and lobs. Your first objective should be to make his advance to the net as hazardous as possible. Therefore, try to keep the ball deep and to his weak stroke. Do not let him hit forcing approach shots from inside his baseline. If you inadvertently hit short and he makes a good attack, do not try to pass him outright. Play defensively instead. Drive or slice low to make him volley up. If you are wide in your court, hit crosscourt to keep him from angling the ball away from you. Crosscourts will help get you out of trouble and keep you in the rally until you get a safe chance to become aggressive. Mix in many lobs with your low shots, especially after his first volleys; since he will be closing in for his second hit, he will be more vulnerable for a lob. If you are winning, continue to use your winning tactics, but be alert for any changes in his.

If you are losing, try to determine whether his good volleys or your bad passing shots are making his net game effective. You may be trying to be too accurate on your passing shots and thus missing more of them than you make. Make him show that he can volley well enough to beat you. If he is not able to, you will not have to pass him outright. You may be able to draw errors, particularly on his backhand volley. Most players have a built-in weakness there just as they do on some ground strokes. At any rate, try to determine why points are going against you, and change your tactics and strategy accordingly. Don't beat yourself. Be a thinking player; if your opponent is to win, make him outthink you and outstroke you.

Play situations

8

Stroke development is only part of the process of learning to play tennis effectively. You not only must hit the ball well, but you also must know where to hit it, where to stand, and when and how to move. This requires that you use and apply your strokes quickly in the many varied situations that develop during a match. In many of these cases you will not have time to think. You will have to act automatically, and hopefully, your automatic response will be the right one. Do not leave everything to chance, however. Through training and practice, you can develop an awareness of each situation as it develops, and this will help establish fixed responses that will enable you to act quickly and properly even when there isn't time to think.

At the beginning of each point, whether you are serving or returning the serve, you have time to set yourself securely into position and even to plan your next shot or two in advance. Once the ball is in play, however, the action often gets so fast and the tactical situations become so varied that following a fixed plan is difficult. You may, for example, find yourself in a backcourt rally exchange in which you are "sparring" with your opponent, hoping to create an opening and an opportunity to attack. But you suddenly may realize that he is already attacking; he already may be on his way to the volley position. In such a situation, there are usually right and wrong ways to respond, but there is no time to plan your moves and shots. Therefore, you must react habitually in the way you learned through practice.

Tactical situations such as these—serving, returning the serve, rallying from the backcourt, going to the net, and playing against a net man—generally are referred to as "play situations." In these situations, experienced players usually follow certain rules of thumb. Several such rules are presented on the following pages of this chapter. They are intended to serve as guides that will teach you to respond properly and automatically to any situation through constant repetition in practice.

You decide to attempt a crosscourt passing shot when hitting from X while your opponent is at volley position Y. Which is your best aim point, A or B? Why?

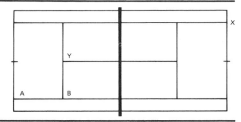

SERVING

1. If you are staying back on your serve, serve from various places along your baseline to give your opponent different angles at which to hit. When serving from the deuce court, stand next to the mark and hit straight down the center line to his backhand. Occasionally, stand closer to the sideline and angle the ball at him. From the ad court, stand close to the sideline to get a good angle to his backhand unless he returns well enough to take advantage of the open court to your right. Occasionally, stand closer to the mark in order to change the angle of your shot. Try to figure out what position draws a weaker return or gives you an easier shot on your next hit.

2. If you are going to the net on your serve, stand where you have the shortest distance to run in order to reach a good volley position. When serving from the deuce court, stand close to the mark. When serving from the ad court, stand a step or so away from the mark. These positions give you a good angle to your opponent's weak backhand and yet give you a short running line to the volley position.

3. If your opponent has an obvious stroke weakness, hit most of your serves to it. If he has an obvious preference for one stroke over another, avoid serving to it. Vary the placement of your serves, however, to keep him guessing; serve wide to his right, wide to his left, and straight at him. Try to keep him guessing and off balance. Do not let him move in confidently to hit.

4. A wide serve toward a sideline may force your opponent out of position and thus give you an opening for your next shot. On the other hand, serves down the middle reduce his angles for making returns. Therefore, consider the advantages and possibilities of each placement and note the trend in the match. You may have to serve wide into one court and to the center in the other. Serving to a weakness in his position (or for strength in your own position) may outweigh the advantage of serving to his stroke weakness.

5. If he handles your hard serves well, it might be because he likes speed. In such cases, do not use your hard serve; use your spin serve instead.

6. It is axiomatic that you are only as good as your second serve. Try to avoid giving your opponent an easy second serve to play. If you are missing a large number of hard first serves and he is attacking your second serve, hit your first one more softly to get more of them in. Put more spin on the ball even if it means giving up any chance for "aces."

7. Good depth is important on your second serve. If the ball is landing short, change the toss or the position of the racket on the ball at contact. Carry

the ball up on the strings more to change the trajectory and the height of the ball as it crosses the net.

8. On slow courts, the serve is much less effective as a preparatory shot for a volley than it is on fast courts. If your opponent handles your serve well and gives you difficult first volleys, it may be wise to stay back and wait for a ground stroke approach.

9. Your first serve prepares you much better for a safe volley than your second one does. Try to get a good percentage of them in, even if you must hit with less than maximum speed. Don't let your opponent feel that he can move in confidently for an easy ball, however; hit hard enough to keep him guessing.

10. When you go to the net on your serve, stop running, make a split-stop, and get ready to move to the ball as your opponent makes his hit. If he suddenly moves in quickly to play your serve earlier than he usually does, adjust your steps accordingly. Adjust your steps to correspond to the speed of your serve, too. After a "cannonball" you may have time for only two or three steps. This will put you in "no-man's land," but you can risk being caught there after a hard serve. A slow serve may allow time for four or five steps and let you get up close to the service line for your first volley. In either case—whether in "no-man's-land" or on the service line—move up to the ideal volley position after you make your first volley if you can continue the attack.

11. If your opponent consistently makes good, low returns, you should vary the number of steps you take before making your check. Occasionally, stop short and let his low returns bounce up to you for a ground stroke. If he notices your tactics and starts to return deeper, start moving in all the way again to intercept his higher returns with volleys. Try to keep him guessing about your intentions; don't give him a consistent target, such as the service line, to aim for.

12. When you serve wide to your opponent, stand off center on the line that bisects the angles of his returns as he makes his hit. If he returns a wide serve with a sharply angled crosscourt shot, move in perpendicular to the line of flight of the ball to intercept with a volley.

RETURNING THE SERVE

1. When returning the serve, the important thing is to get the return in play, not necessarily to hit a winning point. Adjust the length of your swing, therefore, to permit consistently good returns. Against a fast serve, a half-swing with a firm grip and wrist and lots of body rotation should be adequate. On slower serves, you may have time for a longer, fuller swing.

2. When receiving the serve, stand on the line that bisects the angle formed by two imaginary lines drawn from your opponent's position to his widest possible aim points in your court. If you have a preference for either a forehand or a backhand, however, move away from that side a bit to lure him into hitting to your preference—leave a slightly larger opening on the side you prefer.

3. Your position with respect to your baseline should vary depending on your opponent's serving ability and on your ability to handle his serves. Against

a hard server, you may have to stand behind the line a step or two; against an easier serve, you can be up closer. You may have to change your position between the first and second serves. Experiment during a match to find out where you can stand and handle the serve well.

4. As you wait for the serve, grip your racket firmly and use the left hand to hold the racket head up and to help move it on the backswing. Be light and bouncy in your stance, ready to move just as the server meets the ball. Raise your eyes to see the ball leave his racket. Relax or loosen up a bit just before contact so that you will not be starting from a static, stationary position.

5. Against a fast serve, standing back behind the baseline will give you more time to react, but it will also require you to cover a wider angle. Experiment to see which is to your advantage—standing in close to take the ball early with a short swing or standing back farther and using a fuller swing.

6. If your opponent's high-bouncing spin serve bothers you, experiment to see how you can handle it best. Taking it high on the bounce while it is still rising and slicing it back may be your best play, especially if he is a good volleyer. If he doesn't volley well or if he doesn't come up at all after his serve, it may be best for you to stand back farther to let the ball come down so you can swing more fully. Try both methods to see which works best for you in each particular match.

7. Returning the ball down the line may give your opponent a chance to angle the ball away from you on his next shot. A crosscourt return, on the other hand, may be to his stronger stroke, but it will prevent him from hitting a sharply angled shot to the apparent opening. Consider both possibilities and use whichever plan you think will work best.

8. If you have trouble returning the serve, you may do better to always return the ball in the direction from which it came. You will not have to adjust for the angles of incidence and reflection, and you are likely to return more consistently.

9. If your opponent consistently follows his second serve to the volley position, stand in close enough to take the ball on the rise and high on the bounce. Here you have a convenient target, the service line. Try to make your shot land somewhere along that line. To prevent him from angling the ball sharply away from you on his first volley, hit down the center to narrow your opponent's angles. If you make him hit a half volley, anticipate a short, weak return. Move up into the court a step or two to be ready for it.

10. When you hit a crosscourt return, aim for the short corner if your opponent has come up to volley. A deep crosscourt shot is likely to be within his reach. When you hit down the line, you can aim either short or deep.

11. Use your most consistent shot (crosscourt or down the line) more often than your uncertain shots, and almost always on a crucial point. When you cannot afford to lose the point, do not try a risky shot; do what you do best. Tactically speaking, if you have been mixing up your shots, it might be wise to play the percentage shot (the one you do well) on a crucial point; if you have been playing the percentage shot, it might be wise to mix in a surprise shot.

12. If you intend to follow your return to the volley position and your opponent has served deep, the percentage shot will be down the line because

it will bring your line of good position closer to you. On these returns get a running start by stepping toward the ball with the foot that is closest to it (the right foot in the case of a forehand).

13. When you have to step sideways to reach a wide ball, step perpendicularly to the line of fight of the ball. This will give you a shorter distance to reach than if you move parallel to the baseline. Avoid making a wide crossover step on wide shots if you can; skip sideways and hit with an open stance, if necessary, to maintain balance and good position for a recovery.

14. If he does not follow his serve to the net, return deep to make your opponent go backwards to hit a backhand, unless a crosscourt is necessary to insure getting back to good position. Because he has to hit a backhand from behind his baseline, he will lose all the advantage he had in serving. At least you will be starting the rally on even terms. These returns do not have to be hard drives. Medium-paced shots with a safe net clearance are adequate.

15. Occasionally, make an obvious move forward as you get ready to receive your opponent's second serve. It may even be a fake move, but it should make him think you are moving in confidently to attack his serve. Try to tease him into taking chances and hitting better than he normally can.

16. Whenever possible, attack on the second serve. Try to put pressure on the server immediately. Start to control the rally even then.

RALLYING FROM THE BACKCOURT

1. Your best position for backcourt play, one from which you can move to play both offensively and defensively, is one step behind the baseline. Stand either directly behind or to the left or right of the center mark in order to be on the line that bisects the angle of the widest spots to which your opponent can hit.

Fig. 8.1 When your opponent hits a ground stroke, you should be on the line that bisects the angle of his possible returns. Note that in this instance, when he hits from his right alley, you should be approximately one step off center to your right. Note also that if you were at the net, you would be off center in the opposite direction.

2. If your opponent has a "built-in" weakness, play to it; if not, try to move him to create a weakness—make him weak in position. Do not play to his weak stroke so often that he gets enough practice to improve it during the match. It may be wise to save your attack against his weakness for a crucial point or at least for a crucial shot within a point.

3. Control the depth of your shots by controlling their height. The height above the net for each shot should vary depending on the purpose of your shot and your position. To hit deeper, you may have to hit higher as well as harder.

4. When your opponent gives you a short shot, try to get it high on the bounce so that you can hit it down. Move up to the ball quickly.

5. Sometimes it may be necessary to play to your opponent's strong stroke in order to find an opening on his weak stroke. This happens when he consistently runs around his weak backhand, for example.

6. When you hit a strong shot to your opponent's weakness, anticipate a weak return; move up into your court a step or two so that you will be in position to take advantage of his weak return.

7. Sometimes a player's strongest stroke is not his steadiest. Consider the percentages. Trade him "one for two." Your opponent's flashy, hard forehand may be more erratic than his slower, steady backhand. You might be able to gain advantage by playing to a strong but erratic shot.

8. When you are forced to run toward a sideline and you feel you may have trouble getting into position for the next shot, hit a slow, deep crosscourt. Crosscourts get you out of trouble and keep you in the rally by bringing your line of good position closer to you. They also lure your opponent into hitting parallel to the far sideline, so you will not have to chase wider than that line to reach his shot. (See figure 8.2.)

9. Do not hit down the line unless you see an opening there or feel you can return to your line of good position, ready for the return.

Fig. 8.2   When hitting from an alley, your best shot for regaining good position may be crosscourt, to make your opponent hit from the opposite alley. You then bring your line of good position (line 1) closer to you, as shown in the photo.

10.   Do not be a "baseline hugger." If your opponent hits deep, you may have to move back to hit a ground stroke. Try to avoid having to hit a half volley or a pickup shot from the baseline.

11.   Notice how your opponent hits the ball. If he cuts or slices it, or spins it in any way, you will have to play the bounce accordingly. A slice motion with a lofted trajectory will cause his ball to slow up on the bounce (it may even bounce vertically). A slice motion with a fast, forward trajectory will cause his ball to skid low on the bounce. If he is hitting at a low ball and drags his racket across the ball, it will bounce in the opposite direction from which his racket is traveling.

12.   Consider the wind; be aware of whether it is gusty or calm. Vary your play accordingly. When hitting against it, hit to a medium level for depth. When hitting with it, hit to a lower level. When the wind is blowing across the court, make allowances for it when aiming close to the sidelines. Certain wind conditions may give you a "downwind" shot. Maneuver your opponent and lure him into giving you a chance to attack with that shot. Drop shots and lobs are more effective against the wind than with it.

13.   For most effective use of the drop shot, consider three factors: (1) your distance from the net, (2) your opponent's position and distance from the net, and (3) the direction in which he is moving. The safest time to drop-shot is when you are relatively close to the net and he is far from it. Aim for the short corner of the net that he is farthest from. If he is moving to get back to position as you hit (if has not checked), you may be able to hit a short shot behind him and "wrong-foot" him.

GOING TO THE NET

1.   Go to the net only when you are able to use your strong stroke from a position on or inside your baseline. Hit to your opponent's weak stroke or to where he is weak in position. Hit strongly enough to make him return the shot from behind his baseline.

2.   Play your approach shots aggressively but carefully enough to make a good percentage of them. Do not beat yourself. Make the other player prove that he can hit passing shots well enough to beat you.

3.   When your opponent hits short to you, try to take the ball high on the bounce (above the height of the net, if possible) so that you do not have to hit up. You will be able to hit hard with a greater degree of safety if you are hitting at waist height or higher.

4.   At the intermediate level of play, your best approach shot will usually be forehand down the line, deep to your opponent's backhand. At higher levels of play, the best approach shots are usually down the line whether to his forehand or backhand) to reach a good volley position.

5.   If you do have to take the ball low on your forehand, a slice down the line to your opponent's backhand can be an effective shot. Hit down and across the ball to give it some sidespin, which will make it bounce low and wide to his backhand.

6.   After your hit, move in quickly to be ready and waiting on the line that bisects the angles of your opponent's possible returns. Stand off center

Your partner is having difficulty with your opponents' hard serves and he is unable to keep his returns away from the opposing net man. Which is the best position for you when your partner is receiving, A, B, or C?

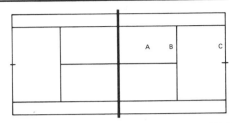

to the right or left, depending on his position, and get in as close to the net as you can. Stop running wherever you happen to be when he meets the ball, pause momentarily, and then move again to reach his return. Move up to the ideal volley position for your second hit. (See figure 8.1.)

7. When your opponent forces you to hit at a low ball on your first volley, do not attempt to return his shot with a winner every time. It may be best to play the shot as another approach shot, that is, deep to his weak stroke or to where he is weak in position.

8. Notice how your opponent hits the ball. If he cuts or slices it, the backspin will cause the ball to deflect downward off your racket. Make allowances; do not aim too closely to the net or a line.

9. If your opponent hits a sharp-angle passing shot, move perpendicularly to the line of flight of the ball in order to reach it.

10. Look for "giveaways" to your opponent's intentions. Study his mannerisms; observe his stance, the tilt of his racket, and how he lines up for certain shots. He may even glance in the direction he intends to hit. These physical movements may help you anticipate his shot. Anticipation is simply a matter of imagining yourself in his position and figuring out what you would do in a similar situation. Evaluate the chances of success of each of his choices and try to recall his preferences on previous points.

PLAYING AGAINST A NET MAN

1. When you are in the backcourt and your opponent is coming in or is already at the net, use your location as a guide in the selection of your shot. If you are hitting from inside your baselines, you may be able to pass him with one shot. If you are hitting down the line, your shot can be either short or deep. If you are hitting crosscourt, however, your shot will have to be to the short corner; a deeper shot is likely to be within his reach. However, if you are very close to the net, you might be able to hit hard enough to get the ball past him even though it is within his reach. In this situation, too, you can aim either deep or short.

When you are hitting from behind your baseline, do not try for a one-shot winner every time. Instead, wait for a safer chance to pass, a shorter ball that you can put away. Hit low to make your opponent volley up; aim for a short corner. When you are very deep and on the defensive, lob.

2. If you are hitting from a location close to a sideline and you intend to continue the rally rather than end it with your shot, your best shot will be

A returned the last ball. Now the opponents send it between the partners. Should A or B take it? Which one should take it if A and B were at the baseline?

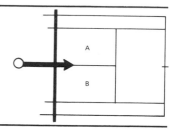

crosscourt. It will prevent your opponent from angling his volley sharply away from you as he aims to the apparent opening. Trick him into volleying parallel to the far sideline; his shot, then, will not bounce across the sideline.

3. When you force your opponent to hit at a low shot, especially a half volley, anticipate a weak, short return. Move up into your court a step or two so that you can take advantage of it.

4. When your opponent gives you a short ball, move in quickly to get it high on the bounce. Try to get it at waist height so you will not have to hit up to make your ball clear the net.

5. When you are forced to hit at a very low ball and have to hit up, aim for a short corner. Your chances of passing are not too good, so you should play to get a safer chance on your next hit. Try to make your opponent move to volley up. If he has a weak backhand volley, this is the time to play it. If you can hit down the line to his backhand, a soft, medium-high lob is often effective. You do not have to get the ball over him from this position. Making him hit at a very high backhand volley will get you out of trouble just as well. But from this position, your best shot may be a crosscourt lob; you will be able to use the long dimension of the court and therefore be less likely to lob too long.

6. Try to keep your errors on passing shots to a minimum. Make your opponent prove that he can volley and smash well enough to beat you. Don't beat yourself.

7. Against a net man, you usually have your choice of three shots: (1) a low shot to make him volley up; (2) a winning passing shot; and (3) a lob. Mix them up to keep him guessing and to keep him off balance.

8. Use your best, most trusted passing shot much more often than you do your uncertain one; use it on virtually all the crucial points.

If, for example, you prefer to hit down the line rather than crosscourt off your backhand, do not hit crosscourt unless you have to. If you like to slice rather than drive to hit a backhand low and short, play it that way. Use the shots you feel you do best.

9. As you play your opponent's approach shot, he usually will be back too far for you to lob over him. When he closes in for his second volley, however, he will be more vulnerable to a low, offensive lob. For these shots, disguise your stroke to make it look like a drive; then, at the last second, loft the ball over him.

Drills for practice

9

In tennis, playing only in game situations will not give you enough practice to improve regularly in the many separate parts of the game. An entire match, for example, may give you only three or four chances to use your dropshot on your opponent, to smash his lob, or even to pass him with purposeful deception. You will need many more attempts to be able to correct faults in these strokes, and you will need a lot of practice time to learn new strokes and shots.

To improve these separate skills, you should practice them with drills designed for specific purposes. Several popular and beneficial drills are described here. To use them most effectively, you first must find a practice partner who is as serious about his game as you are about yours and wants to spend as much time practicing as you do.

Regardless of your level of play, certain skills are essential for effective performance. You must serve or return the serve on every point, and you have to be able to keep the ball in play in a rally. In addition, you must be able to play effectively at the net position and prevent your opponents from doing so. These skills are basic,and you should practice them often.

You also should practice to develop the various separate parts of your game that need special attention. You may need extra work on smashing or lobbing, on half volleys, or on sliced approach shots. Analyze your game carefully to determine where you feel inadequate, and arrange to practice longer and harder in those areas. Practice the basics and "specials" as often as you can, preferably daily. Plan your schedule and your court time so that you can follow each practice session with play. Sometimes you should play for practice in a situation in which you will not care about the consequences of missing, so you will feel free to risk shots you are unsure of. At other times, you should play seriously and attempt to win. Practice is not a substitute for competition; it is only a supplement to it. You will learn to play better by playing more, so your training schedule should include both practice and play.

RALLYING FROM THE BACKCOURT

Use this drill as a warmup to begin each practice session. It will prevent you from hitting carelessly as you loosen up.

With both you and your practice partner standing in the backcourt, one of you starts a rally by bouncing and hitting the ball. The person assigned to practicing offensive shots tries to move the other, attempting to make him run along the baseline to create an opening and to draw an error. He should use whatever mixture of shots he can. Drive or slice and hit short and deep, crosscourt and down the line. Net play is not permitted; both of you must stay in the backcourt.

Meanwhile, the other person plays defensively. He retrieves as well as he can and uses the proper shot to get out of trouble and regain good position. After a suitable time has passed, reverse your roles.

THE DEEP GAME

A variation of the preceding drill provides practice at controlling the depth of your shots. Rally as you did in the first drill, but now try to place your shots into your partner's "deep area," which is the area between the baseline and a line drawn across the court six feet inside the line. The rally ends and you lose the point if your shot does not land in this deep area. His shots must

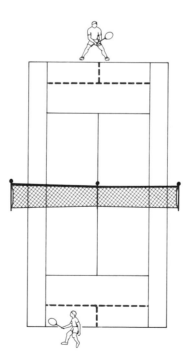

Fig. 9.1 Sketch shows how court should be marked for "deep game" drill. A ball is "good" only if it lands in the area between the baseline and the dotted line in front of it. To practice for even greater accuracy, draw in a short line at each center mark to provide target squares for crosscourt shots.

land only in your deep area, too. Net play is not permitted. Score as you would in table tennis, numbering points consecutively to twenty-one.

Variations

The preceding drill can be made more difficult by placing your shots to each other's backhands. Draw in another line, extending the center mark toward the net up to your deep area boundary. You can require your partner to hit to your backhand deep area; if he cannot do so well enough to give you backhand practice, he may first be permitted to play your shots with his forehand so that he can feed balls accurately for you to practice your backhand. You can reverse your roles after a suitable length of time.

In a second variation, you and your partner can practice hitting alternately to each other's forehand and backhand deep areas. In all variations, the emphasis is on both left-to-right control and control of depth. The purpose of the drill is to develop steadiness and accuracy as well as pace and depth.

GOING TO THE NET AND DEFENDING AGAINST A NET RUSHER

Again, begin a rally from the backcourt; this time one of you is the attacker, and the other is the defender. The attacker is permitted to go to the net any time he strokes a ball from a position inside his baseline. The defender tries to keep the ball deep to make the attacker hit from behind his baseline so that he cannot go to the net.

In a typical exchange, the attacker moves forward to play a short return from the defender and tries to make an aggressive approach shot, usually to the defender's weak stroke.

When the attacker runs forward to volley, the defensive player tries either to pass him outright or to keep the ball low while waiting for a safer chance to pass. He uses the kinds of shots he would use in match play: top-spin or flat drives, slow slices and dinks, and defensive lobs.

THREE-SHOT TENNIS

In a variation of the preceding drill, the play is more specific. The attacker starts at his baseline, makes a self-drop, then runs forward to volley. The defender returns the ball as well as he can. The rally ends after the attacker's first net shot. He "wins" the rally if his net shot bounces either across a sideline, beyond the baseline, or twice inside the service line (as it would if he made an accurate drop volley). The defender tries either to pass the net man or to hit low to his feet. He may even defend with a lob. But no matter how he defends, the emphasis of the drill is on avoiding errors rather than on hitting for "winners."

Experienced players can vary this drill by having one player start a rally with a feeder shot that he hits short purposely to permit the other player to make an approach shot and a net attack. You can use this version of the drill to practice attacking an opponent's weak stroke (usually the backhand) or to move him to create a built-in weakness if he doesn't have one.

SERVING AND RETURNING THE SERVE

Start by serving in your regular manner, trying to serve effectively enough to draw a weak return. Your partner "misses" if his return doesn't land in your deep area. If he hits well enough, he may be required to hit into your backhand deep area. In either case, there is no rally. This is a serve-and-return practice only.

Soon, after each of you has had his turn making deep returns, the server runs to the net to volley every return, and the receiver then tries to pass him or hit low to his feet. The server makes only one volley or half volley, and the point ends. His volley is "good," and he scores a point if his ball bounces either across a sideline or beyond the baseline. The importance of these three shots—the serve, the return, and the first volley—is highlighted when the drill is restricted to them. This more difficult version of the drill may be called "serve and first volley."

PASSING SHOTS

Have your partner take a position at either of the short corners where the service line meets a sideline. From the backcourt, hit to him, to his feet if possible. One of you should begin the rally with a feeder shot. For the most part, your partner's shots should not be fast. They should be placed to dif-

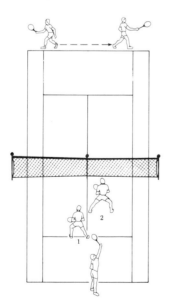 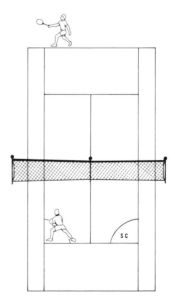

Fig. 9.2 For advanced serve-return-volley-pass practice, the server runs to the net to volley, first from the "T," then from the ideal volley location. Diagram shows him properly off center for each of his opponent's shots from the alleys.

Fig. 9.3 For passing shot practice, a player stands at one of the short corners so his partner can practice shots to that area.

ferent sections of your court to permit you to practice a variety of shots, all aimed in his direction. Some should be crosscourts, for example; others should be down the line. After a suitable period of time, have him move to the other short corner so you can practice hitting in that direction.

After several practice sessions, when you can hit accurately, change the drill slightly. Have the volleyer stand at the "T," the intersection of the service line and the center line. The other partner should continue to hit from the backcourt to one or the other of the short corners. You may agree to hit consecutively to one, alternately to each, or randomly to either corner. From his new location, the volleyer gets many chances to practice volley footwork; he learns how to lunge, reach, and stretch to reach the sidelines.

VOLLEYING THROUGH MIDCOURT

This drill provides practice in volleying to reach the net position as well as volleying from that position. Both you and your partner begin by standing at your center marks. One of you starts a rally with a bounce-and-hit and moves forward two steps afterward. He tries to hit deep into the opponent's court and straight at him. The other player then returns and moves forward two steps. He tries to hit to his partner's feet, which are now two steps inside the baseline. Continue to rally, with each of you moving forward two steps after each hit. The object of the drill is to draw an error on your partner by forcing him to hit at a low ball that he, in turn, cannot hit back to you low. Hopefully, you will get a high ball that you can hit aggressively to draw an error.

Each of you should carry an extra ball in your nonplaying hand so that you can start another rally from any location after a miss.

In addition to using the drills outlined here, you and your partner should practice whatever areas of your game you feel need attention. The routines for tournament players usually include work on lobbing and smashing, on volleying for quickness from close range, on making the first volley (from the "T"), and on making sharply angled volleys from a position very close to the net. All of these shots and those described in the drills are required at one time or another in match play, so they should be part of your training program.

Doubles strategy

10

Doubles require different shots and different tactics and strategy than singles. In singles, backcourt play often wins, particularly at the intermediate level. In doubles, however, net play, or at least a combination of net and backcourt play, is usually the winning style. Backcourt play is used only for defensive purposes, and even then only as a temporary measure. Team players almost always try to get into a good volleying position from which they can hit the ball through the middle between their opponents or angle it sharply off to the sides for a winner. Since both teams go up to the net as soon as possible, rallies are short; they usually consist of a serve, a return of serve, and one or two volleys. Lobs and overhead smashes are used when necessary, but generally serves, low drives, and volleys are the principal strokes employed.

Net play is so essential and effective in top-flight play that both teams station a player at the net at the beginning of every point. The server's partner stands six or eight feet from the net, close enough to his sideline to reach it with a crossover step if he has to. In play, he also stretches toward the center with a crossover step to reach balls there. In addition, he moves back when necessary to make a play on all lobs aimed at his half of the court.

The server usually serves from a position that permits the shortest running distance to the volley position. He almost always runs up to volley after serving, in much the same way a singles player does; he runs, checks as the opponent hits, then moves to reach the ball. He starts from the center of his half of the court—midway between the mark and a sideline—and runs straight in from there to join his partner. His objective is to serve well enough to draw a weak return, one that can be volleyed aggressively by either him or his partner.

The receiver's partner usually stands in the vicinity of the service line in his half of the court. From this position he moves forward a step or two to volley aggressively if his partner's return is low, or he holds his position and plays defensively if his opponents are attacking the return of serve.

In top-level play, the receiver usually stands close enough to his baseline (sometimes even inside it) to permit him to play the ball on the rise and thus get a good start to the volley position. He usually runs in to volley immediately after his return. He tries to hit to the feet of the server (who is also running in to volley) in order to draw a weak return that either he or his partner can hit aggressively. Consequently, all four players are often at the net at the same time, trying to score with quickness, accuracy, and speed.

These are the starting positions and plans in top-level doubles play. Each team tries to get to the net as soon as possible because the volley position is the attacking position. Even though you cannot serve or volley as well as ranking players, you ought to begin now to get accustomed to these tactics.

SERVING

Hit a large majority of your serves at three-quarter speed to the receiver's backhand, with enough spin to insure getting a good percentage of first serves in. Try to avoid having to serve an easy second ball that the receiver can play confidently and aggressively. Vary your serves occasionally. Hit a slice to the receiver's forehand or a hard, flat one straight at him often enough to keep him guessing about your intentions.

If you have confidence in your ability to serve and volley, run to the net to join your partner. If the return of serve is high, make an aggressive volley. Aim either to the feet of the opposing net man, into his alley, between your opponents, or deep or short to the receiver, depending on his location (deep if he has stayed back, short if he has moved forward).

If the return of serve is low enough to prevent you from attacking on your first volley, your situation is a bit more difficult. As you prepare to volley after you have served, you must notice, in the periphery of your vision, whether the receiver is advancing to the net behind his return or is staying in the backcourt. If he stays back, aim deep down the middle if you feel you can keep the ball away from his net man. If the receiver has angled his return, however, you may be able to angle your volley and so begin to create an opening between your opponents. If the receiver comes to the net after his return, anticipate how far he will be able to advance before you hit and aim at that spot, to his feet. If the return of the serve is low, at your feet, the opposing net man may be poaching (in his partner's territory). Angle your volley to keep the ball away from him. Aim either deep or short to the receiver, depending on his location.

If the receiver has to lunge sideways to reach your serve or has to jump away from a close ball, he will not have a running start to the net. If you see that he is approaching the net in spite of his difficult position, aim your volley deeper than you normally do. If you aim to your usual spot, the ball may bounce nicely to him for an aggressive ground stroke, and you and your partner may find yourself on the defensive.

If you cannot serve well enough to draw weak returns consistently, it may be best for you to stay back after your serve and wait for a safer chance to go to the net. From your position in the backcourt you will seldom be able to win outright with a drive unless, of course, one of the opponents is out of position. Usually, you will have to rally patiently and hope to draw an error or a weak shot that you or your partner will be able to attack.

THE SERVER'S PARTNER

If your partner is serving, stand in the middle of your half of the court and slightly forward of midway between the net and the service line. This is only your starting position, however; you must be prepared to move from it. If the serve is placed wide, you must move to cover your alley as the receiver moves to play the return. If the serve is placed down the center line, you can move in that direction a step or so and try to intercept. If the serve is weak and short and the receiver moves in to return aggressively, you may have to back up a step to gain more time to play the ball. If the serve is strong and deep, you can often safely extend the range of your reach toward the center by poaching. Hold your starting position until the receiver is in the act of playing his shot. When you feel he is committed to hit in a certain direction, dash across and intercept. Any balls you can intercept while in this position should be aimed at any opening away from or between your opponents, or at the opposing net man's feet.

RECEIVING THE SERVE

If you can attack on your return of serve, do so. If the server stays back, hit deep to keep him back, unless he doesn't like to volley or cannot handle low, short balls. If he has come in to volley, your objective should be to make him

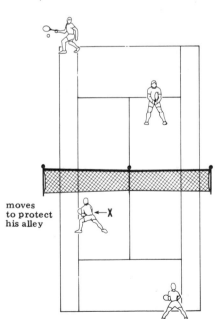

moves
to protect
his alley

Fig. 10.1   When you are at the net and an opponent is hitting from an alley, you must move to protect that alley.

hit at a low volley or a half volley. The sooner you make your play on the return, the less time the server has to run forward (he will make a split-stop just as you hit the ball). Stand in as close as possible, so that you can hit the ball early enough to make him stop in the vicinity of the service line, a location from which he probably will not be able to hit an aggressive volley. Your exact position should depend on the speed and bounce of the serve and on your ability to handle each particular kind of serve. Play the ball on the rise, if you can, to get it back to him quickly and hit your crosscourt return at a sharper angle. In addition, the close-in position gives you less distance to run when you follow your return in to volley.

The majority of your returns should be either drives or slices, whichever prove more effective. Top-spin drives that curve downward to the receiver's feet will be difficult to volley, but slower slices or "dinks" to his feet will give you more time to move in to a good volley position and, therefore, may be good percentage shots. A hard, flat drive to change the pace of your return may disconcert your opponent and should be used often enough to keep him guessing.

If you can't return the serve with an attacking shot, it may be best to stay in the backcourt and rally until a safer chance to move in develops. Hit the ball deep to an opposing backcourt man or low to the feet of either the weaker volleyer or the player farther from the net.

Lob to change the pace of your returns, to prevent a net man from moving forward aggressively, and to return serves that are too difficult to handle any other way. Most of your lobs should be aimed over the server's partner, because he is likely to be closer to the net than the server. If, however, the server runs in quickly enough to be the same distance from the net as his partner, a lob to the corner he has vacated may be your best play. His forward momentum may make it difficult for him to stop and reverse his direction to play the lob. Furthermore, you will be lobbing along the long diagonal dimension of the court and thus have a larger area into which to place your shot.

If the server does not follow his serve to the net, there is no need for you to play the ball early. Stand, then, wherever you can best handle it. For hard first serves you may have to stand three or four feet behind your baseline. For easier second serves you may be able to move in a bit. You may also have to alter your position, depending on which of the opponents is serving. One may serve more effectively than the other, and so you may stand deeper for one than for the other.

Whether you are attacking or defending, whether you are playing the ball early or late, you must keep the ball away from the opposing net man, who is hoping to intercept and attack (unless you are so close to him when you hit that he cannot defend himself). If he does poach and intercept your returns, aim a few into his alley to keep him in place. The more he bothers you, the more you should play in his direction. Drive low into his alley so that he cannot attack. When he jumps around to distract you, or fools you with fakes and feints, surprise him with a lob.

If you can handle the serve well enough, and if you volley well enough, move in to join your partner in the attacking position as you make your return.

If the net man is unusually aggressive in doubles play, is it better to concentrate on avoiding him or hit in his direction? Where should you position yourself to receive a hard serve?

If the served ball is comfortably within reach, you may be able to stroke it while moving toward the net. Such a running start will enable you to get closer to the net for your next shot, so you should hit that way whenever possible. If you have to stretch or lunge to reach the serve, however, you will get a slower start to the net. It may be best, then, to stay back on your return and wait for a safer time to attack and move in.

THE RECEIVER'S PARTNER

When your partner is returning the serve, your position should vary according to how well he can handle the serve. If he can keep the ball away from the opposing net man and hit deep to a backcourt server or short to a net-rushing server's feet, you may be able to play safely at the net. Stand a step inside your service line (this is back farther than your position when your partner is serving) and in the middle of your half of the court. From this position you can move forward a step or two to volley aggressively if the opponents are forced into a defensive shot, or you can hold your position and defend yourself if a bad service return permits the opponents to attack you. If you do intercept a weak shot, aim either to any opening away from or between your opponents or at the opposing net man's feet. Whenever you can, "pick on" the opposing net man.

If the serves are so effectively that you don't feel safe at the net (your partner can't return effectively), stand at the baseline and wait for a safer chance to attack. From here, you and your partner can play defensively while trying to create an opening or draw an error from your opponents. Don't try to drive the ball through them unless you are very close to the net. Instead, use a mixture of low drives, slices, and lobs to force them back or to draw weak, short volleys. When you and your partner get one, move in, hit hard, and advance to the net together.

A very simple plan often helps to avoid confusion in this situation. Make an agreement with your partner to let the hitter decide whether his team is to go up and attack or not. The hitter can best evaluate his potential for making a good shot. His partner can read his intentions, then abide by the decision and react accordingly. You can thus avoid the embarrassing situation of having one player move forward while the other stays back to play defensively. In doubles, this one-up, one-back formation is usually a weak one, especially if there is some uncertainty about the hitter's intentions.

PLAYING TOGETHER FROM THE BACKCOURT

When you and your partner play from the backcourt against opposing net men, your usual plan should be to mix defense with attack. The two of you should divide the court in half at the center line, each standing at the base-

Under what circumstances in doubles play should the receiver's partner re-main at the baseline?

---

line in the middle of his half. Your positions should change, however, as you anticipate certain shots of your opponents. If one of them is hitting at a half volley (which you should hope to make them do), one of you should move into the court a step or so in anticipation of a short return. If an oppo-nent is smashing from a sideline, you should both move away from his di-rection slightly to be properly off center.

When they hit short, you have an opportunity to attack. Here, if you are hitting at a low ball, a soft slice, or dink, may be your best play. Played low and softly, it can cause an opponent to hit at a very low volley or half volley. Having had time to run in after your soft slice, you are likely to get a high volley that you can hit aggressively. If you are hitting at a high bounce from the vicinity of your service line, your best play may be a hard drive hit directly at an opponent to win on sheer speed.

When you are hitting from the vicinity of your baseline, your best play may be a drive, either a top-spin shot meant to dip low to a volleyer's feet or a low, flat shot into an alley. Your choice of direction here may be deter-mined by several factors: you may choose to hit to the weaker player, to the lowest part of the net (over the center strap), to the feet of the player farther from the net, or to the alley of the player most likely to be anticipating a centered shot.

Another frequent possibility is the lob. When you are very deep and the opponents are in good volleying position, the lob may be your only hope of staying in the rally. Here, too, you should aim each lob for a definite reason. If one of your opponents is standing too close to the net, lob in his direction. If one player is shorter than the other, he may be easier to lob over, but if one is obviously weaker at smashing, he should get most of the play. You may sometimes wisely decide to lob crosscourt in order to have the long, di-agonal dimension of the court along which to hit. A final choice to consider is a low, half lob to the backhand of the weaker opponent. Such a shot need not be intended to fly beyond the reach of your opponent. Instead, the plan may be to let him hit at the ball and make an error or, at least, a weak, short return.

PROTECTING YOUR PARTNER

When rallying from the backcourt when your partner is at the net, your main consideration should be to protect him, while trying to draw weak shots from your opponents. You can protect him in several ways: (1) keep the ball away from the opposing net man and deep to the opponent in the backcourt, (2) hit low, to your opponents' feet, if both opponents are at the net, and (3) lob defensively if they have made a good attack.

The same shots you use to protect your partner often draw weak returns that he can put away for winners. In a sense, then, you play to protect your partner while also trying to "set him up" for a kill. Remember: although he

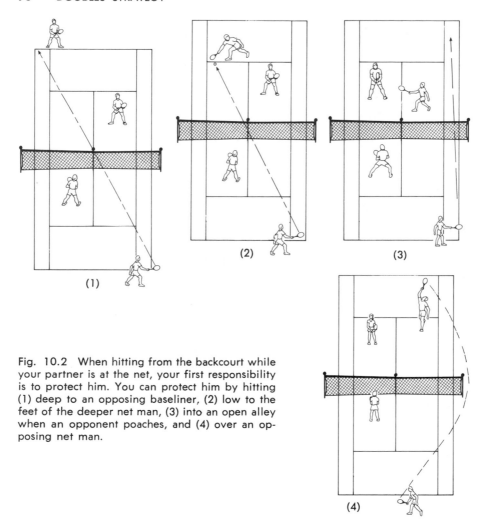

Fig. 10.2 When hitting from the backcourt while your partner is at the net, your first responsibility is to protect him. You can protect him by hitting (1) deep to an opposing baseliner, (2) low to the feet of the deeper net man, (3) into an open alley when an opponent poaches, and (4) over an opposing net man.

is in the attacking position, he is also in a position to be attacked. Hit your shots deep or low to keep him out of trouble.

PLAYING TOGETHER AT THE NET

When both you and your partner are in volley positions, you should move up or back, left or right, depending on the positions of your opponents and the kinds of shots you expect from them. When an opponent is hitting from close to the center line, your primary concern should be to protect the center of your court. When an opponent is hitting from close to a sideline, however, both of you should shift sufficiently toward that sideline to protect against both a shot into the alley and a shot toward the center.

When an opponent is hitting from a short, wide angle, you and your partner must cover both a shot along the line and a sharply angled crosscourt shot. To do so, whoever is farther from the hitter should move forward and toward the center line (to intercept or at least discourage the angle shot), while the partner should move to protect the alley. He may even have to drop back slightly to be in position to retrieve a lob aimed diagonally across the court. Remember to protect against a sharply angled return after you have hit a ball to your opponents.

DEFENDING YOURSELF

Playing effectively from the net position while your partner is in the backcourt requires an understanding of doubles tactics and position play. You must be alert to move forward to play offensively when possible and to hold your ground or even to retreat and play defensively when necessary.

When your partner is hitting from behind you, turn to watch him except when he is serving. By watching him hit, you are likely to get an early indication of his intentions and his aim point. Then, by looking ahead of the ball into your opponent's court, you can determine their positions and intentions. You can then get an earlier start to move into position to play their shot than if you had watched only your opponents for their reaction to your partner's shot.

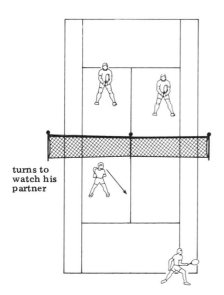
turns to
watch his
partner

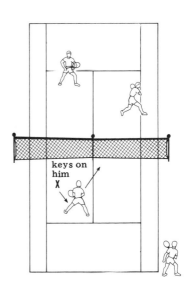
keys on
him
X

Fig. 10.3 When you are at the net and your partner is hitting from behind you, turn to watch him long enough to determine his intentions, as in (a). Quickly, then, turn to look ahead of the ball to the opponent making a play on the ball, as in (b).

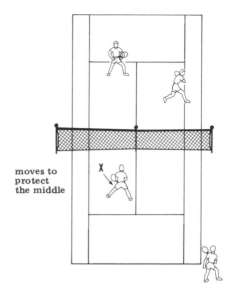

moves to
protect
the middle

Fig. 10.4   When you are at the
net in doubles and your partner is forced wide to play a
ball, move toward the center
to help defend that area against
an opponent's return.

If, for example, you see your partner moving very wide to play a shot, you can move toward him a step or two to help cover the big hole created by his move. Move to leave two smaller holes (one on each side of you), either of which you can cover better than the one larger one. And if you see your partner setting up for a lob, immediately start back to a defensive position. On all except the very deep lobs, your opponents would like to smash at you if you are caught in the volley position or in no-man's-land. Don't let that happen. Hurry back to a good defensive position. As you run back, however, try not to be moving as they hit. Stop and defend yourself, wherever you are, even if you are in bad position.

If your partner is somehow forced into a difficult situation, anticipate his weak return and plan to move for defense. If, for example, you sense the opponents moving in to the net together, move back a step or two in case your partner can't protect you. The opponents are probably closing in to pick on you. Don't let them. Move back to put some space between yourself and them so you will have time to defend yourself. In this situation, you are likely to be safer behind the service line than up very close to the net, even though you will probably be forced to hit at a low shot from back there.

TEAMWORK

A few simple rules agreed on beforehand will enable you and your partner to play together smoothly and avoid many uncertain moves and positions. When you are at the net together, for example, and the opponents drive a ball down the middle within reach of both of you, let the player who has hit the last ball in the rally take this one. If still another ball comes between you, let him take that one also. Most players establish a rhythm when they make successive hits. And, conversely, most players feel "cold" when left out of a rally. Whenever possible, let the player who has established his rhythm play the ball.

Have you and your partner agreed on which of you will play balls down the center under various circumstances? If the situation is not clear and both of you call "mine," who should make the play?

An exception ought to occur if one player is definitely stronger and more reliable than the other. In such a case, the better player ought to play the shot whenever possible.

A similar situation often develops when you and your partner are in the backcourt. Here, however, you will probably have more time to think. The player on the left side, whose forehand is in the center, ought to play the ball with that stroke. Most players are weaker on the backhand than on the forehand. If this is true for you and your partner, avoid a backhand whenever you can; if possible, let the stronger forehand play the shot.

When you and your partner are at the net and your opponents lob to the center, whichever of you has the stronger overhead ought to play the shot. However, there may be some uncertainty about whether that player can get into position or not. In such a case, voice calls can often settle the matter. "Yours"; "I have it," or "you take it"—these are examples of helpful calls that promote teamwork. Agree beforehand with your partner that a call is never rescinded and that when more than one call is made, the first one is in effect. Ignoring calls, or overruling a previous call with another one, can be disastrous.

If the opponents succeed in lobbing beyond your reach, retrieving is often difficult. Normally, the man to whose side the ball is hit is responsible for all balls hit in his direction. However, if either of you has moved in too close to the net (which is probably why the lob got over you), the other may be in a better position to make the retrieve, even though his run diagonally across the court is longer than his partner's run parallel to the sidelines. He may have an easier play on the bounced lob when running sideways (and half facing the net) than the other player, who is in full retreat with his back completely turned to the net.

As this play is made, you and your partner will have to exchange sides. The net player either moves across to be in position to volley from the side left vacant by his partner or retreats to the baseline to play defense. His choice is determined by the kind of shot the retriever is making. If he can protect his partner with a low shot to an opponent's feet or with a deep one to a backcourt player, your team may choose to play in the one-up, one-back formation. If the retriever is in trouble, however, it may be best for you to give up the net position.

UNUSUAL FORMATIONS

Occasionally, it may be to your team's advantage to use formations slightly different from the conventional ones that have been described. If, for example, you have a weak serve and backhand that your opponents attack, particularly when you serve from the left court, your partner can protect this weakness by standing to the left of the center line as you serve. Seeing him in this attacking position at the net, the receiver will try to keep the ball away from him. When he does so, he will hit to your forehand. All you have to do is move over a step or two across the center mark after serving to defend your right court. From this position you can continue to rally with your forehand by hitting down the line, which is the opposite side of the court from the opposing net man. Your intention is to avoid having to use your weak back-hand.

If you are afraid to go to the net when serving from the left court because of your opponent's effective crosscourt returns, the same formation described above may work. Your partner at the net will be in a position to volley the crosscourt return; consequently, the receiver will very likely return down the line, and you can probably volley these returns with your forehand. Your in-tention here is to block off the receiver's preferred return and to force him into trying a more difficult one.

Another reason for using an unorthodox formation is to enable you to keep your first volley (after you have served) away from a consistently effec-tive poacher. If, when you serve from the right court, for example, the re-ceiver's partner consistently intercepts your first volley (or half volley), hav-ing your partner take a position on the right side of the center line might be a good countermeasure. The receiver will then try to keep the ball away from him by hitting down the line. Meanwhile, you can run forward and to your left to volley the return of your serve from your own left service court. From that location your first volley will almost certainly be out of reach of the receiver's partner.

Formations such as these often can help to cover your weaknesses or to minimize strong shots of your opponents. But the fact that they are not con-ventional indicates that they don't always work. The majority of top players consider them to have inherent weaknesses and to indicate deficiencies by players who have to use them. Nevertheless, they may work and are worth trying if things are going badly.

POACHING

You can increase the effectiveness of your partner's serve by playing agressively in the forecourt. Rather than simply holding your position and playing only balls that are comfortably within your reach, make frequent moves toward the center of the court to increase your range. You don't need to dash across the court wildly and leave your alley exposed (though this sometimes is effec-tive). Instead, you can simply skip sideways a few feet as the opponent makes his hit. From this new position closer to the center line you can then reach across the line with a crossover step to intercept the return when you think it is safe to do so. From that same position you are still able to step back toward your alley to cover about half of it if you have to.

Your poaches are more likely to be successful when they are made in re-sponse to various cues given inadvertently by an opponent. A player's stance, or his backswing, or even his eyes often reveal his intentions. Watch your opponent carefully; study him and try to relate any unusual mannerisms or points of form to shots he plays concurrently. If he appears to be having difficulty handling a particular shot such as a high-bouncing serve to his backhand, or a fast one hit straight at him, or a half volley from midcourt, he is not likely to be able to place his return accurately. Usually, troublesome shots such as these are played carefully and safely to the conventional aim points, away from the closest net man. Knowing this, you should be able to dash across the center line to intercept many of those returns.

Skill in poaching lies in being deceptive. You often can confuse an opponent by varying your methods—by standing perfectly still sometimes before making your moves and by shifting, swaying, and faking in place at other times. In the first instance, you occasionally can surprise him by sneaking across to intercept a normally good return. In the second instance, you can often distract him or cause a poor shot or even trick him into hitting straight at you as you hold your ground after making a fake move.

When an opponent is hitting from close to your alley, you may deceive him in still other ways. At times, make an early, obvious move toward your alley as if to protect it at all cost. Your opponent, seeing this, will certainly hit crosscourt rather than into your alley. Knowing this, you can wait until the last split second, then dash across the court to intercept his return. Or you may appear to be leaving your alley open by failing to move toward it. Then, as your opponent hits to the apparent opening, the vacant alley, you can move in that direction to intercept.

But you should also occasionally move clear across the center line to intercept, even though you will sometimes be fooled by a return down your unguarded alley. One way of preventing this is by having a prearranged signal with your partner (usually an open or closed fist given behind the back to prevent the opponents from seeing it) and using it to indicate when you intend to poach into his territory. Then, he runs up to the net toward your alley to cover for you in case the receiver has anticipated your move. Skill in poaching lies in concealing your intentions and in waiting until the last split second to dash across the court. Moving too early, before the receiver has committed himself, often results in a lost point. Until you gain experience, you may be wise to poach only on the first serve when the receiver can return less effectively than he can on easier second serves.

Conditioning

11

To prepare properly for serious competitive play, you ought to condition yourself physically so that you can play energetically for the entire length of a match. You can attain such a properly conditioned state through regular performance of special exercises designed to develop and maintain special qualities needed in match play, namely, endurance, quickness, agility, and strength. True, a great deal of play is itself a conditioner for more play. However, you are not likely to be able to spend as much time as it will take to get conditioned that way. A better plan, therefore, is to design a training program specifically for the purpose of developing and maintaining the needed qualities more quickly.

For maximum effectiveness and efficiency a training program should be based on three widely accepted principles: specificity, overload, and interval training. The theory of specificity holds that any attribute—quickness, speed, strength, or endurance—is developed best by practicing the actual skills or movements used in competition. This means you should spend considerable time practicing the actual footwork and racket movements used in match play. In addition, you should run for conditioning in a manner similar to the way you run in match play.

As you exercise and begin to tire, remember to use the theory of overloading. Simply stated, it holds that you must tax your muscles by performing exercises that require an output beyond that needed in the actual contest. This kind of conditioning will create a reserve that you can tap in an emergency without hampering your ability to maintain a steady pace throughout a match.

The third principle to apply in your program, interval training, suggests that you alternate periods of vigorous effort with rest periods. These periods should follow in quick succession. Then, by gradually increasing either the length of the work period or the speed at which you do the work, you will increase the amount of work done. The result will be increased endurance for that kind of work.

Have you planned a personal progressive conditioning program designed to improve your tennis game? How have you utilized the three principles of specificity, overload, and interval training?

Finally, remember that your program will be only as strong as its weakest part. You must establish regular living and training habits and get an adequate amount of sleep and rest. Your diet is important, too. Make it a sound one with a regular intake of the proper amount of protein, carbohydrates, fats, vitamins, and minerals. Avoid rich, starchy foods and sweets that offer only quick energy and very little nourishment. Disregarding any of these items will minimize the effectiveness of your conditioning.

RUNNING

Tennis is primarily a leg-heart exercise; therefore, running is one of the best means of conditioning. Running for conditioning should consist of alternating periods of vigorous effort and rest periods following in quick succession. Sprint for thirty yards, for example, and then repeat at small time intervals, either resting or running slowly between sprints. Then gradually increase the length of time you sprint or decrease the length of the rest period. Do this routine regularly for a period of several weeks, and you will increase your endurance for that kind of running.

A more effective plan is to supplement your sprint-and-jog program with running that is more realistic for tennis. Run around a gym, a track, a battery of courts, but as you run, make the kind of quick stops and starts and changes of direction that occur in match play. For example, run for ten yards, make a split stop, then lunge first to your left, then to your right, by making crossover steps as if reaching for wide volleys. Recover to the ready position, sprint forward ten yards, then repeat the crossover steps. Continue this way around your exercise area until you are well beyond the point of initial fatigue.

If running space is not available, make crossover steps alone in whatever space you find adequate. Or you may prefer to run in place for ten or twelve counts, then hop to a ready position and do crossover steps to simulate net-play conditions.

Another good running exercise, one designed for the development of agility and endurance, is "spot running." Run in place slowly for about fifty counts (one count each time a foot touches the ground). Then run as fast as you can for fifty counts with your feet barely leaving the ground. Alternate running fast and running slowly. As you develop strength and stamina, gradually raise your knees higher in the slow part of the exercise, and gradually lengthen the time of each running period. Early in your program you may need to rest a short time between running periods. For variety, move sideways to your left and right in the fast part of the exercise.

In all of these running exercises, try progressively to increase the amount of work you do before resting. Also, always force yourself to continue beyond the point at which you begin to feel the effort. The work that you do when you are tired conditions you for that kind of work.

AGILITY

Unquestionably, the ability to move quickly and easily is an asset in tennis. Fortunately, there are several ways to exercise to develop agility, and you should try all of them to find which you prefer and want to use regularly. The crossover steps described earlier, when done at maximum speed, serve well for this purpose. Rope skipping, too, is a good agility exercise. Running up and down stairs and running backward, then forward, with quick stops and changes of direction are also helpful.

One of the better agility drills may be performed on a court. Stand on the center service line, and then skip sideways to your right and touch the right sideline. Quickly reverse direction and skip to your left until you reach the left sideline. Continue to move sideways back and forth between the sidelines, moving as fast as possible.

An additional agility exercise can be done in a very limited space. Stand in a stride position with your left foot advanced slightly. Hop around in a circle on your left foot while keeping your right foot in place, with the right heel off the ground. After tiring, rest briefly and repeat, moving your right foot around in a circle. As you develop strength and stamina for this exercise, spread your feet wider; the wider your stance, the more difficult (and beneficial) the exercise.

STRENGTH IN THE HAND, WRIST, AND FOREARM

The simplest and most efficient way to develop strength in your hand, wrist, and forearm is to rally a ball against a wall or backboard with a covered racket.

Fig. 11.1　To develop strength in your hand, wrist, and forearm, rally against a backboard with a covered racket.

The added weight of the cover and the air resistance caused by it will teach you to hold your racket firmly. As you do so, you will be developing the kind of strength you need to play well.

If you are able to volley the ball against the wall, do so. This, of course, will require—and build—more strength than when you let the ball bounce before hitting it. In both exercises, use your regular grips, the same grips you use for forehands and backhands, ground strokes and volleys on the court.

To develop the wrist action you need for serving, serve the ball against the wall with your covered racket. Here, you will feel the air resistance even more than on ground strokes or volleys, but as you learn to use your wrist and fingers to force the racket through, you will be improving your ability to generate racket speed when serving.

FLEXIBILITY

Tennis requires more than the normal amount of flexibility at the hips and lower back. A few simple exercises designed to help you develop and maintain flexibility in these key areas can be done in a very small space.

For the first one, simply stand erect and, keeping your knees straight, bend at the waist and extend your hands as far toward your feet as you can. Do the movement slowly to avoid soreness. Hold your maximum reach position until you begin to feel stretch pain, then return to the upright position and repeat ten or twelve times. As you begin to feel more limber (after several days) do the movement faster to make your flexibility more applicable to tennis movement.

A second exercise is similar, yet different enough to be considered in addition to the previous one. Stand facing a wall or fence. Place your hands flat on the wall. Gradually move your feet away from the wall, but keep your heels on the floor. When you feel a pull on your calves, stop your backward movement. Hold that position until you feel stretch pain, then relax and repeat.

For an exercise that is more applicable to tennis, stand in the conventional ready posture (as if to volley at the net) and make a crossover step to your right with your left foot. Grasp your left ankle with both hands and hold that position for four or five seconds. Recover to the ready position and repeat the exercise on the other side. As a variation, reach beyond your foot with the opposite hand each time you cross over. Extend your reach and hold until you feel stretch pain.

To maintain flexibility at the trunk, lie flat on your back with your arms and legs spread and resting on the floor. Raise your left leg, twist and turn at the trunk, and place your left foot next to your right hand and directly opposite your shoulders. Hold that position for eight or ten seconds, then return to the starting position. Repeat the exercise on the other side. Try to keep your trunk flat on the floor so that you feel stretch pain at the trunk.

To stretch the muscles of your lower back, lie on your back with your feet and head flat on the floor. Raise your right leg, bend the knee, and draw it toward your chest. Grasp your shin in both hands and force your knee against your chest. Lower and straighten the leg and repeat the exercise with your left leg. As a variation, draw both knees into your chest and press them against the chest with your arms.

WEIGHT TRAINING

When done regularly and properly, weight training will lead to the maintenance of flexibility in key joints and develop strength in key muscles.

For tennis, the best procedure with weights is to use a light or moderate load that you can move quickly for a number of repetitions. Lift daily to increase the number of repetitions but continue to use only as much weight as you can move quickly.

Barbell Press

Stand comfortably holding a medium-weight barbell (20-30 lbs.) under your chin at chest height, with your palms turned upward. Press the weight upward quickly until your arms are fully extended. Return to the starting position and repeat until tired.

Barbell Curl

Stand holding the bar in front of your thighs, arms straight, and hands spread to shoulder width, palms facing away from your body. Raise the bar to your upper chest by flexing your biceps. Lower the bar to the starting position and repeat.

Simulated Serve

Hold a 5-pound dumbbell in your serving hand in a position directly overhead, with your arm straight. Bend your arm at the elbow to lower the weight behind your back as low as you can while keeping your upper arm vertical. Pull the weight straight up forcefully until the arm is again completely extended. Lower the weight and repeat the exercise until you are tired.

Sideways-overhead Swing

With a 5-pound dumbbell in each hand, stand in a normal position with your arms relaxed at your sides. Straighten your arms and extend them sideways and upward until the weights touch overhead. Return to the starting position. Next move your arms forward and upward until the weights are directly overhead. Repeat the exercise, alternating sideways and forward lifts, until you are tired.

ABDOMINAL STRENGTH

Many experienced athletes believe that the degree of firmness in their stomach muscles is an accurate indication of their overall condition. Two simple exercises for keeping your stomach muscles toned are described here.

Bicycle Riding

Sit on the floor with your legs extended together in front and your heels held just off the floor. Draw one knee in toward your chest and then quickly extend that leg to force your knee and foot away from your body. While you extend your leg, draw the other knee in toward your chest, then quickly extend and straighten that leg. Continue to alternate, drawing your knees in and extending them and moving your feet in a circular pattern.

"V" Sit

Sit on the floor with your legs together extended in front of you. Raise both feet off the floor, lean back slightly at the waist, and raise your arms above your head. Balance yourself on your buttocks and lower back while your legs are slanted upward at a 45-degree angle.

Fig. 11.2   Two simple exercises for increasing fitness for competitive play. (1) The "V" Sit. Balance yourself on your buttocks with legs and upper body off the floor as shown. (2) Kangaroo Jump. Jump upward and forcefully draw both knees up and toward your chest. Make several consecutive jumps until tired.

Situps with a Twist

Lie on your back with your hands clasped behind your head, your knees flexed, and your feet flat on the floor. Contract your stomach muscles and raise your upper body to the sitting position. When you are erect, twist your body so that your left elbow touches your right knee. Return to the lying position, sit up, twist in the other direction, and touch your right elbow to your left knee. Continue to alternate left and right elbow touches to your knees.

LEG STRENGTH

Stand with your back flat against a wall and your heels on the floor about six inches from the wall. Bend your knees to lower your body while keeping your trunk straight and your back pressed against the wall. Lower to only a half knee-bend position and then straighten your legs to raise your body. Continue to bend and straighten your knees until you are tired.

Glossary

Ace. An outright winner by virtue of speed or placement as opposed to a winner scored on an opponent's misplay (used most frequently to refer to a served ball that the receiver cannot make a reasonable play on).

Ad. A contraction of the scoring term "advantage"; refers to the first point won from deuce.

Ad court. The service court into which a server must serve when the score is "advantage."

Alley. The area between the singles and doubles sideline on each side of the court (the singles court is made 4½ feet wider for doubles by the addition of the alley).

All-court game. A style of play that combines net play with baseline play.

American twist. A kind of serve in which overspin and sidespin are applied to the ball.

Approach shot. The shot after which a player moves into the volley position (usually applied to a ground stroke).

Backcourt. The area in the vicinity of the baseline as contrasted with the area close to the net (the forecourt).

Backhand. A stroke made from the side of the body away from the player's hitting arm.

Backspin. Spin imparted to the ball when the racket moves in a plane that is downward from a line drawn perpendicular to the hitting surface.

Backswing. The prepatory phase of the stroke in which the racket is carried back from the ready position to prepare for the forward swing.

Baseline. The line 39 feet from the net and running parallel to it at either end of the court.

Baseliner. A player who prefers to remain in the backcourt and attempts to win by using his ground strokes.

Break. To win a game served by an opponent. Break point refers to a point that, if lost by the server, results in his losing that game.

Bye. A pass through the first round of a tournament to the second round without having to play a match. Usually occurs when the number of entrants is not an even power of two, and is awarded by chance in the drawing.

Cannonball. A hard, flat service in contrast to a slower spin serve.

Center mark. The mark in the center of the baseline. It is an equal distance from the sidelines and is meant to indicate the server's permissible locations; he may stand anywhere between the mark and the sideline.

Center service line. The line under the net and perpendicular to it that serves as one of the boundary lines for the service courts.

Centerstrap. The strap at the center of the net that holds the net securely at the required height—3 feet.

Chip shot. A ground stroke made slowly to apply underspin for control and accuracy (a variation of the chop).

Chop. A ground stroke in which the racket is drawn sharply down against the back of the ball to impart backspin (a variation of the chip and synonymous with "cut").

Close. Moving in closely to the net in preparation for a "kill" shot on the interception of the opponent's return.

Crosscourt. Hitting the ball diagonally over the net and across the court from one sideline to the other.

Cut stroke. A stroke in which the racket hits the ball a downward, glancing blow to impart backspin.

Deep area. The area within and close to the line being used, i.e., the baseline on ground strokes and volleys, the service line on the serve.

Deuce. The score of a game when each player has won three points or when the score is tied after that point. Also the set score when the number of games won by each player is five or when the games are even after that point.

Deuce court. The service court into which the server must serve when the score is "deuce."

Dink. A soft, delicate shot in which the ball has little pace.

Drop shot. A soft, delicate shot intended to barely clear the net and to bounce close to it.

Fault. A served ball that is either hit illegally or does not land within the proper service court.

Fifteen. The first point won by a player.

Five. A scoring term indicating that number of games won by a player. Also used in social play as a contraction of fifteen.

Flat service. A serve in which the ball has little or no spin. Used mainly as a first serve in top-flight play.

Foot fault. A served ball declared illegal because of violation of the rule pertaining to the location of the feet when serving.

Follow-through. The part of a stroke occurring after contact.

Forcing shot. Usually used synonymously with approach shot to refer to the shot after which a player advances to the net. Also means a shot that places an opponent in difficulty because of either speed or placement.

Forecourt. The area of the court between the service line and the net.

Form. The manner in which a player strokes the ball. Usually applied to the total pattern of a stroke.

Forty. The third point won by a player in a game.

Game. A unit of scoring awarded to a player when he has won four points and is two points ahead of his opponent.

Ground stroke. A stroke made after the ball first hits the ground, in contrast to a volley, which is made before the ball hits the ground.

Half volley. Hitting the ball on the short hop, immediately after it bounces.

Kill. A putaway, a ball hit so hard or placed so accurately that the opponent cannot possibly return it.

Let. A replay of a shot or a point that usually occurs on a served ball that lands in the proper service court but touches the net as it sails across. Also refers to replays for interference or misunderstanding between players and officials.

Lob. A ball lofted high into the air, usually used against a net man.

Love. A scoring term used to designate no score, or zero, for a player.

Love-game. A game in which one player or team failed to score a point.

Love-set. A set in which one player or team failed to win a game.

Match. The term used when referring to the complete contest. May be the best two out of three sets or the best three out of five (in baseball, it's a game; in track, meet; in tennis, a match).

Match point. A point that, if won by a player, will make him the winner of the match.

Midcourt. The area midway between the sidelines and close to the service line.

Mixed doubles. Doubles play in which a man and a woman (or a boy and a girl) team up to oppose another man and woman.

Net game. A person's technique for play in the forecourt, his volleys, half volleys, and overheads.

No-man's-land. The area between the baseline and the service line. A player caught here is vulnerable to balls landing at his feet.

Overhead (smash). A shot played against a lob, usually hit much like a serve with an overhead swinging motion.

Pace. Synonymous with speed, used to refer to the rate of travel of the ball through the air after the bounce.

Pass. To hit a ball so that it flies out of reach of a volleyer.

Passing shot. A ground stroke intended to elude a net man.

Placement. A shot placed accurately to cause an error by the opponent or to win outright by virtue of accuracy.

Poaching. Used to describe the manner in which a doubles player extends the range of his reach by moving into his partner's territory to make a play.

Rally. A series of good hits made successively by both players. Also refers to the practice procedure in which players hit continually back and forth.

Service line. The line drawn across the court 21 feet from the net and parallel to it on both sides.

Set. A scoring unit awarded to a player or a team that has won (a) six or more games and has a two game lead, or (b) six games and the tie-breaker played at six-all.

Set point. A point which, when won by a player, gives him the set.

Short ball. A ball landing far short of the baseline, in the vicinity of the service line.

Slice. A stroke that imparts backspin to the ball.

Slow court. A rough surfaced court on which the ball bounces relatively slowly.

Spin. The action imparted to the ball by hitting it obliquely.

Thirty. A scoring term, the second point won by a player.

Top spin. Spin imparted to the ball when the racket moves in a plane that is upward from a line drawn perpendicular to the hitting surface.

Twist. Usually refers to a kind of serve in which the ball spins and takes a high bounce.

Volley. A ball hit before it has touched the ground.

Appendix: Questions and answers

TRUE OR FALSE

t F   1. On ground strokes, your backswing should start soon enough and be made fast enough to permit you to pause and wait before starting your forward swing. (pp. 5, 6, 14)

t F   2. On the backhand ground stroke the upper body should be facing the net at the moment of impact between the racket and the ball. (pp. 17, [photo] 15)

t F   3. Skipping sideways is recommended as the best way to move to reach very wide balls in the backcourt. (pp. 36, 37)

T f   4. On the overhead smash your position relative to the ball at contact should be determined, in part, by your distance from the net. (p. 44)

T f   5. When jumping to reach a deep lob the hitter jumps from the right foot and lands on the left foot. (p. 44)

T f   6. The swing for a half volley should be shorter and more controlled than for a full-length drive. (p. 45)

T f   7. In doubles the more the net man bothers you by poaching, the more shots you should aim in his direction. (p. 75)

t F   8. When going to the net after a ground stroke play all volleys from the same location from which you made your first "check." (p. 65)

T f   9. On the recommended spin serve, there is a sharp angle between the racket handle and the hitter's forearm. (figs. 3.3, 3.6)

T f   10. Elbow action is used as one of the main sources of power on the backhand ground stroke. (pp. 14, [photo] 15)

T f   11. Careful placement of the front foot is recommended as an aid to good balance on ground strokes. (pp. 10, 13)

t F   12. For maximum control on ground strokes hitters are advised to pull the racket across the line of flight of the ball. (pp. 8, 9, 17, 18)

T f   13. In doubles the receiver's position should vary as the effectiveness of the opponent's serves vary. (p. 74)

t F   14. Crosscourt passing shots should be aimed at the deep corner. (p. 65)

t F   15. In doubles the server's partner's best chance to poach occurs on serves wide to the receiver. (p. 74) t F   16. In doubles the receiver's partner should stand in the vicinity of the service line regardless of how well the receiver can handle the serve.   (p. 76)

t F   17. In doubles when the return of serve is hit low to the server's feet his first volley should be hit directly at the opposing net man.   (p. 73)

t F   18. In singles, serve from the same location along your baseline regardless of whether you are going to the net or staying in the backcourt.   (p. 59)

t F   19. The swing for the overhead smash is identical to the swing for the serve. (p. 42)

t F   20. When running to reach a wide ball adjust your speed from slow to fast to enable you to hit while moving.   (pp. 10, 19)

T f   21. In doubles, when both partners make a voice call on a shot the first call made should be in effect.   (p. 81)

T f   22. In doubles when you are at the net and your partner is forced into a difficult position behind the baseline, you should begin to move back to take up a defensive position.   (p. 80)

t F   23. In doubles the server's partner must stand on the opposite side of the center line as the point begins.   (pp. 81, 82)

t F   24. As you run in to volley after your serve, run fast enough and long enough to ensure getting out of "no-man's-land" regardless of how hard your serve is.   (p. 60)

t F   25. The recommended way to put top spin on the ball is to turn the wrist and forearm at contact to roll the racket face over the ball.   (p. 7)

The Continental Grip:

T f   26. is recommended for use when serving.   (p. 21)

T f   27. does not require a change from forehand to backhand.   (p. 2)

T f   28. is used for volleys in advanced play.   (p. 30)

t F   29. puts the palm in line with the hitting surface.   (pp. 2, 30)

T f   30. is used for most half volleys.   (p. 45)

When at the net in doubles when your partner is hitting from the backcourt, you should:

T f   31. turn to look for an indication of his intentions except when he is serving.   (p. 79 [photo] 79)

t F   32. hold your position at the net regardless of your partner's position. (p. 79, 80)

T f   33. move toward your partner when he has moved wide to play a shot.   (p. 80, [photo] 80)

t F   34. hold your position at the net when your partner lobs.   (p. 80)

T f   35. look ahead of the ball into the opponents' court to determine their positions.   (p. 79)

On volleys:

T f   36. the left hand is used to help move the racket during the backswing.   (p. 31)

T f   37. the length of the backswing varies depending on the hitter's distance from the net.   (pp. 31, 35)

T f   38. a crossover step provides maximum reach for wide shots.   (p. 34)

T f   39. fast balls hit directly at a player can be handled best on his backhand. (p. 34)

t F   40. the racket is always held firmly to provide a crisp hit.   (p. 33)

Serves that are consistently misdirected to the left can be corrected by:

T f   41. placing the racket more toward the nose of the imaginary face on the ball.   (pp. 27, 29)

T f   42. swinging across the line of flight of the ball from left to right.   (p. 29) t F 43. tossing the ball farther in front (toward the net). (p. 29)

T f 44. changing your stance to make your body face more to the right. (p. 22)

T f 45. make your swing resemble that of the American twist serve. (p. 26)

The receiver in singles:

t F 46. is not allowed to make a fake move as the server prepares to hit. (p. 62)

t F 47. should make a crossover step on a wide serve to avoid hitting from an open stance. (p. 62)

t F 48. should use his most consistent shot except on a crucial point. (p. 61)

T f 49. should attack on a weak second serve. (p. 62)

T f 50. should move up into his court a step or so if he has made the server hit at a half-volley. (p. 61)

The receiver in singles:

T f 51. should stand on the line that bisects the server's angles. (p. 60)

t F 52. should drive every return, especially against high-bouncing spin serves. (p. 61)

T f 53. will not have to adjust for the angles of incidence and reflection if he aims to the direction from which the serve came. (p. 61)

T f 54. can decrease the angles of the server's first volley by aiming for the center of his court. (p. 61)

T f 55. should use his most consistent shot more often than an uncertain one. (p. 61)

Recommended uses for the ground stroke slice are:

T f 56. to return a high-bouncing spin serve. (pp. 46, 61)

t F 57. to cause the ball to bounce crazily and so fool the opponent. (p. 46)

T f 58. as an approach shot during a rally. (p. 46)

T f 59. as a rally shot while waiting for a chance to attack. (p. 47)

t F 60. as a fast, crosscourt passing shot when hitting at a low ball. (p. 60)

COMPLETION

61. Placing the base of the index finger against the back plane of the handle guides the player into the (*Eastern forehand*) grip. (p. 1)

62. When a player is facing the net as he swings he is hitting from (*an open*) stance. (p. 4)

63. In all except top-level play most players have a built-in weakness, and it is usually on their (*backhand*) side. (p. 51)

64, 65. The (*backhand, crosscourt*) is the basic shot in baseline play. At the beginner's level of play it is used to sustain the rally. Intermediate and advanced players, however, must be able to use it to (*control* [*or win*]) the rally. (p. 51)

66. Very high lobs should be allowed to bounce before making a play on them for the following reason (*they are dropping vertically and so will bounce vertically, consequently, the smasher doesn't have to retreat*). (p. 44)

67. In doubles, when rallying from the backcourt while your partner is at the net, your main objective should be to (*protect him while hoping for a weak shot*). (p. 77)

68. Jumping to the right foot while serving is an effective technique for the following reason: (*adds body motion to swing*). (p. 28)

69-72. The four check points recommended for use to trace the racket path during the serve are: [(a) *knee*, (b) *fence*, (c) *back* and (d) *ball*]. (pp. 24, [photo] 23)

73, 74. Good servers use wrist action and wrist adjustments in their serves. The wrist action is for (*power*); wrist adjustments are for (*control*). (p. 21)

75, 76. Quick adjustments recommended for control of volleys are made in the wrist on the *(forehand)*, and in the elbow on the *(backhand)*. (p. 35)

77. In top-level doubles play the receiver's partner usually stands *(in the vicinity of the service line)*. (p. 72)

78. When volleying, an opponent's shot with excessive backspin will deflect *(downward)* off your racket. (p. 65)

79. At the intermediate level of play, the best approach shot is usually a forehand drive placed *(deep to the opponent's backhand)*. (p. 64)

80, 81. In doubles lobs should be aimed at either *(the weaker player)* or *(the player caught out of position)*. (p. 77)

82-84. Three aim points recommended for the serve are [(a) *wide to his right;* (b) *wide to his left;* (c) *straight to him*]. (p. 59)

85. The ideal location for the volleyer, with respect to distance from the net is *(halfway between the net and the service line)*. (p. 55)

86. The ideal location for the volleyer, with respect to distance from the sidelines is *(bisecting the angle of the opponent's possible returns)*. (p. 55)

87. A lob is likely to be more effective when played against an opponent's first volley than when played against his approach shot for the following reason: *(he will be closing in to volley and so will be closer to the net)*. (p. 66)

88, 89. Poaching in doubles is likely to be more effective on the *(first)* serve than on the *(second)* one. (p. 83)

MATCHING

Match the descriptions on the left with the one best stroke or shot listed on the right.

(10) 90. four or five steps, followed by a check (pp. 55-60)

(9) 91. may be aimed either short or deep regardless of the volleyer's location (p. 65)

(7) 92. player loosens his grip and relaxes his wrist at impact (pp. 33, 46)

(5) 93. the ball is stroked gently on the short hop, and the swing resembles a drive despite its name (p. 45)

(6) 94. the swing sometimes resembles a ground stroke motion, other times, a volley motion (pp. 40, 41)

(1) 95. the hitter jumps backwards and lands on his left foot (p. 44)

(2) 96. should be aimed to the short corner if the volleyer is in good position and in the proper location (p. 65)

(3) 97. two or three steps followed by a "check" (pp. 55, 60)

(4) 98. the hitter makes either wrist or elbow adjustments while using a "no-change" grip (p. 30)

(8) 99. the hitter protects his body by using this stroke (p. 34)

1. overhead smash

2. crosscourt passing shot

3. server's approach to net after a fast serve

4. volley

5. half volley

6. defensive lob

7. dropshot and drop volley

8. backhand volley

9. down-the-line passing shot

10. server's approach to net after a slow serve

ANSWERS TO EVALUATION QUESTIONS

*No answer

Page	Answer and Page Reference
6	*Self-testing item The speed of the backswing. (p. 6)
9	The timing of the swing and the position of the wrist. (p. 7 and Fig. 1.4) Upward. (p. 6)
18	To hit a high shot. (p. 16) When hitting at a low ball. (p. 16) To hit to your left. (p. 17)
28	*Self-testing item
39	*Self-testing item A ball more than six feet away from you. (pp. 37, 38) 1. A recovery step with the right foot. (Fig. 5.1) 2. Planting the left foot. (pp. 4, 39)
42	The defensive lob is high enough to allow time to recover into good position. (p. 40) The offensive lob is meant to barely clear the volleyer's reach. (p. 41) To your opponent's backhand side. (p. 42) When the lob is very high and when smashing under difficult wind and sun conditions. (p. 44)
46	Less forceful. (p. 45) No; it's the volley grip. (p. 45) Yes (p. 45)
49	The hitter can pull the rising ball down. (p. 46) *Self-testing item
53	*Self-testing item
59	B, because a shot to A would be within his reach. (p.65)
65	C (p. 76)
66	B (p. 81)
76	Hit a mixture of crosscourt and alley shots. (p. 75) Three or four feet behind the baseline. (p. 75)
77	When your partner cannot return effectively, that is, away from the server's partner. (p. 76)
81	*Self-testing item The player who first called "mine." (p. 81)
85	*Self-testing item

Index

All-around game, 50-51
Approach shot, 48-49

Backhand ground stroke
  arm action of, 17
  backswing, 14
  balance during, 18
  body action during, 17-18
  elbow action of, 17
  eye action during, 18
  finish of, 18
  follow through on, 17
  forward swing of, 16
  grips for, 12
  hitting stance for, 13-14
  knee action during, 16-17
  point-of-contact, 17
  timing of, 17
  two-handed stroke, 18-20
  wrist position for, 13, 17
Backspin
  on backhand slice, 46
  on drop shot, 45
  on drop volley, 43, 46
  on forehand, 47
  on lob, 46
  on lob volley, 41
  on volley, 41
Backswing
  on backhand, 14
  on forehand, 5, 6
  on half volley, 45
  rhythm of, 4, 5, 6
  on running approach, 49
  on serve, 24

  on slice, 46
  on smash, 42
  speed of, 4, 5, 6
  on volley, 31, 32, 33
Balance
  on backhand drive, 18
  on forehand drive, 10-11
  stepping properly for, 10

Conditioning
  for agility, 86
  for flexibility, 87
  interval training, 84
  overload in, 84
  running for, 85
  specificity in, 84
  for strength, 86, 87, 88, 89
  weight training for, 88
Contact point
  on backhand, 17
  cushioning effect during, 8
  on forehand, 7
  prolonging on forehand, 9
  prolonging on volley, 31
  on serve, 22, 25, 27, 28, 29
  on smash, 42, 43
  on volleys, 35
Continental grip, 2, 21, 30

Depth
  control of, 54, 63
Double strategy
  backcourt play, 76, 77
  defending yourself, 79
  net play, 78, 79

changing wrist position for, 31
drag volley, 31
drive volley, 32, 33
drop volley, 33
grips for, 30
length of swing, 35
moving for, 34
placement of, 35
to protect body, 35
ready position for, 31
reducing speed of, 33
snap volley, 32
variations of, 31

Watching the ball, 18
Wrist
action during drop shot and drop volley, 46
action during forehand, 8, 9
action during serve, 25, 27, 29
action during smash, 42
action for top spin, 7
position at contact, 3, 7, 8, 13
position during half volley, 45
position during lob, 40
position during two-handed shot, 20
position on backhand, 13
position on forehand, 3, 8